| DATE | | |
|---|---|---|
| MAY 2 0 1997 | | |
| MAY 2 9 1997 | | |
| JUL  2 1997 | | |
| JUL 2 9 1997 | | |
| AUG 1 6 1997 | | |
| NOV 2 0 1997 | | |
| | | |
| | | |
| | | |
| | | |

# A HEALING FAMILY

*The Oe family*

# A HEALING FAMILY

## KENZABURO OE

With illustrations by
### YUKARI OE

Translated by
### Stephen Snyder

KODANSHA INTERNATIONAL
Tokyo • New York • London

ACKNOWLEDGMENT
The publisher wishes to thank Osaka Gas Co., Ltd., a
member of the Association for 100 Japanese Books, for its
contribution toward the cost of publishing this translation.

Originally published in book form by Kodansha Ltd. in
1995 under the title *Kaifuku suru kazoku*.

Distributed in the United States by Kodansha America,
Inc., 114 Fifth Avenue, New York, N.Y. 10011, and in the
United Kingdom and continental Europe by Kodansha
Europe Ltd., 95 Aldwych, London WC2B 4JF. Published
by Kodansha International Ltd., 17-14 Otowa 1-chome,
Bunkyo-ku, Tokyo 112, and Kodansha America, Inc. Copy-
right © 1995 by Kenzaburo Oe/Yukari Oe. English trans-
lation copyright © 1996 by Kodansha International Ltd. All
rights reserved. Printed in Japan.
First edition, 1996
ISBN 4-7700-2048-1
96 97 98 99   10 9 8 7 6 5 4 3 2 1

# A HEALING FAMILY

EDITORIAL NOTE
These essays were written over a period of
several years, so references to events hap-
pening "this year" may in fact relate to an
earlier date.

With the author's permission, some parts of
the original text have been omitted in this
translation, and the order has consequently
been reorganized to some extent.

# "Bebe" and "Unpa"

TWO YEARS AGO, at our own expense, my wife and I published a collection of our son Hikari's piano compositions. In the afterword, I wrote the following lines which I want to quote here because I feel they give an idea of the nature of his handicap and the meaning that music has for him.

> Hikari was born with a brain abnormality. In a very real sense, one could say he was "reborn" when he underwent surgery to correct this problem. The doctor who performed that operation and looked after him later for many years

was Nobuo Moriyasu, and the piece "Requiem for M" was written on his death. It has a piercing sadness to it that came as a shock to the rest of Hikari's family, music being the only means by which we can fully understand his emotions.

As Hikari was growing up, it gradually became clear that his mental development would be slower than that of other children, but my wife remembers his sensitivity to music from the time he was an infant. When he was barely three, he could already recognize a piece of Beethoven ("Bebe") or Chopin ("Unpa"), which we had playing almost constantly in his nursery. (My wife too, as the young mother of a firstborn child with a handicap, must have found a certain comfort in the music as she sat next to his crib.) In my case, I noticed that he was particularly responsive to birdsong, and rushed out to buy a record of a hundred birdcalls which I played for him with almost manic frequency. This craze of mine was rewarded one day in the woods surrounding our summer cottage when Hikari, who was five at the time, in a voice that exactly mimicked the announcer on my record, suddenly identified a bird: "That's a water rail," he said in the solemn tones of the voiceover—a short sentence that was, in fact, his very first intelligible use of language to communicate with us.

As he got older and began to attend first a special class at his elementary school and later, for his middle school years, a school for the handicapped, his interest in birdsong receded and music came to the fore. Mozart and Bach, along with his first loves, Beethoven and Chopin, became his constant companions. It wasn't until he began learning the piano with Kumiko Tamura, however, that he had a chance to compose his own music. Since his handicap affects his physical abilities as well, Mrs. Tamura did not insist on a lot of fingering exercises; instead, she patiently devised various ways for him to learn to pick out chords and begin to construct melodies, until one remarkable day my wife and I were presented with a page covered with what looked like bean sprouts: Hikari's first composition.

Sitting nearby with a book, listening to his piano lessons, I can feel the best, most human things in his character finding lively and fluent expression; and when I hear the works he has produced performed by Mrs. Tamura and other musicians who have been generous in their support, I feel in awe of the richness of his inner life. Yet this is a life that, were it not for music, would have remained hidden, would have been utterly unknown to me, to my wife, and Hikari's younger brother and sister. I am not someone who believes in any faith, but I find it hard to deny that there is something . . . something akin perhaps to "grace" in this music; indeed, listening to Hikari's music, being exposed to the world beyond our everyday experience in which it seems to participate, makes me appreciate in it the full meaning of this word: not only "gracefulness" and "virtue" but "a prayer of thanks."

Each of the sixteen pieces included in his *Piano Works*

conjures up a certain scene from our family life. To us, and particularly to my wife, it often seems as though we have never stopped to catch our breath since the day Hikari was born; but at least from time to time there have been pauses, moments of calm amidst the frenzy, and, much to my amazement, it is these moments that the music manages to recapture. Some pieces mark specific events: "Graduation," for example, refers to the ceremony to commemorate Hikari's completion of the special course at his elementary school, while "Bluebird March" was written for a student festival at the school he attended later (which is in fact called the Bluebird School for the Handicapped). But not all of the compositions can be linked to a particular date. "Summer in North Karuizawa," for example, is a whole season in our life, and as I listen to a recording of the piece made for us by a pianist friend, I enter once again the space and time of some of our holidays in a cottage there. In my wife's sketchbooks from those summers, among the pictures of the local flowers and plants, are several drawings of our children, and these, together with Hikari's music, bring back that time in extraordinarily vivid detail.

Our younger son, who entered the science program at the University of Tokyo this year, tells me that he wrote a school composition in first grade entitled "Marathon." It seems that during one particular summer—Hikari would have been starting middle school while our daughter was still in elementary school—the three of them ran a "marathon" each morning from our cottage on the hill down through the woods to a small stream formed by a spring next to the tennis courts. As the races shaped up, my daughter was apparently content simply to tag along after her brothers, completely unconcerned about winning. (It is a mystery to me how this little girl full of boisterous laughter can have become the demure young woman who graduated this year from college.) But our younger son was determined to get the better of his brother, eager to be able to return to the cottage to announce his victory to his mother, who would probably have been in the garden transplanting bellflowers or something. Despite some furious finishes, however, Hikari always seemed to win these daily "marathons."

Looking back on it, I realize now that it was during that summer that Hikari reached the peak of his physical development. Soon afterward, he began to suffer from epileptic seizures and put on a good deal of weight, so that he no longer went out to run with his brother and sister when we were staying at the cottage. For Hikari, the joy of running free during those summers, from the time he was ten to perhaps twelve or thirteen, was a high point in his life. Nor did this apply to him alone: for my wife, holding her sketchbook and examining some plant as she waited for the children to return from their race, and for me as well, reading nearby on the porch, those days were the high summer of our life, a season now relegated to the past. The three of us, Hikari prematurely due to his disability, my wife and I in the natural course of things, are now approaching the autumn of our lives, that "painedful" (to use Hikari's word), inevitable, and ever nearer period we all have to endure.

# Scrupulous Humor

ONCE A MONTH, someone has to go to the pharmacy at the university hospital in Itabashi to collect Hikari's anti-seizure medication. We have been doing this for so many years now that it has become an established routine and not something we would be likely to forget. Still, it happened one Saturday that we suddenly realized there wasn't enough medicine left to last until Monday, and I found myself making an unscheduled trip to the hospital pharmacy. Finding it locked and dark, I was standing, somewhat panic-stricken, at the bus stop trying to decide what to do next when an elderly patient out for a walk came up to speak to me. I explained my predicament, and he suggested I try the receptionist in the Emergency Room in the basement, where I was in fact able to obtain a day's supply of Hikari's medicine. For my trouble, however, I also received a rather severe scolding from the nurse in charge, who told me I should make a point of coming sooner next time.

Having learned our lesson, when the end of the month approaches, someone in the family chooses a day—any day but Saturday—and sets out for the hospital. Though the trip takes the better part of a morning, I often volunteer for this duty since I can take a book along and get almost as much reading done as I would in my study. It was on one of these excursions, after waiting nearly an hour in the large dispensary attached to the hospital, that I heard my name, or rather Hikari's name which is on the prescription, being called by the white-robed pharmacist. When I arrived at the counter, he told me that it would take some additional time to prepare the medicine and suggested I go and have lunch while I was waiting. He sounded quite polite and considerate, but having heard some chatter on the loudspeaker that made me suspect there had been some mistake in filling the prescription, I sensed a certain lack of candor in the young man's manner.

Still, I hadn't much choice but to make my way to the hospital cafeteria, a place with which I've been familiar for more than twenty years. As I entered, the peculiar mustard smell in there and the sight of the usual, plain sandwiches brought memories of my son's operation crowding into my head. The room was quite full, but I found a seat in a corner next to three young doctors who were talking quietly as they ate. They were apparently discussing the prospects for surgery on a patient—I couldn't tell if it was an adult or a child—who had a deformity of the brain, and they seemed to agree that the operation was pointless since even if it were successful there was no hope that the patient could ever function as a normal member of society.

As I listened to them, my thoughts turned to a hospital in Nagoya for severely disabled children that I had visited not long before, and in particular one autistic child I'd seen lying on the spotless floor—everything in the ward seemed spick-and-span—with a doctor squatting next to him offering words of comfort and encouragement. The boy was due to have intestinal surgery the next day, and I remember wondering how they had ever managed to discover the source of his silent suffering, and how they would help him cope with the pain of the operation without the benefit of language. The sight had moved me deeply, and while I sat eating my curry I considered trying to convey what I'd seen to the three young men sitting next to me. In the event, I regret to say, I never found the courage to interrupt them, in part because I could sense their weariness, itself a sign of the effort they put into their work.

The following week, Hikari came down with a cold accompanied by a fever, making him miss several days at the vocational training center where he works. On the second or third night of his fever, I woke to hear him coughing violently and went to his room to check. As I looked at his bright red face and watery, staring eyes, I was struck by the realization that my son, whom we so often treat as a child or even a baby, was in fact an independent adult—a young man absorbed at the moment in his own discomfort. His whole body seemed to communicate his desire to be rid of the pain and uncertainty; and as I stood looking down at him, unable to do anything to help, I remembered my experience in the hospital cafeteria, the smoldering anger I'd felt then now flaring back to life. Anyone watching me might have seen my face turn as red as my son's, heard my breathing become as ragged as his. Yet as I continued to watch him lying there suffering like that, my anger subsided; and a short while later, after merely refilling the cup of water by his bed and adjusting his blankets, I switched off the light and returned to my room. This little episode had somehow succeeded in unraveling the knot in my heart from the week before, and I went back to bed feeling at peace.

2

As I have said, our son Hikari didn't really begin his life in this world until after having the operation to remove the lump on his head and cover the hole with a plastic plate. This is something I have written about any number of times over the years. The doctor who performed the surgery and continued to treat him afterward was Nobuo Moriyasu of the neurosurgery department at Nihon University Hospital. What I want to emphasize here, though, is the fact that Hikari wasn't the only one to benefit from the care and healing offered by the doctor; indeed, he served as a healer for our whole family.

Several years ago, shortly after Dr. Moriyasu's death, I received some photocopied pages from his wife. They were from his diary, a daily record of his long years as a doctor written in his strong yet meticulous hand; it was a document that differed, I felt, from the journals of scholars or writers in its extreme practicality. His widow had apparently come across some pages concerning Hikari and me and decided we might be interested in seeing them. The first of the three entries was a single line, buried among a number of other observations, recording the fact that a young novelist had decided, after some hesitation, in favor of surgery for his son. This one line, with its restraint and, perhaps, unstated censure, electrified me. Without the surgery, Hikari wouldn't have survived; and yet this young father had hesitated for some time before giving his consent. The fact was recorded there, incontrovertibly, in Dr. Moriyasu's diary, reminding me yet again that if there is a god, some higher being who judges us, then when my time comes I will be unable to face this being with a clear conscience, condemned in advance by this one piece of evidence alone. Still, the line in the diary contains more than just my guilt, for it also reminds me that by *having* decided, even after hesitating, ultimately I, too, was reborn along with Hikari.

The second entry recorded Dr. Moriyasu's impressions after attending a ceremony for a literary prize I received for *Rouze Up O Young Men of the New Age!*, a book about life with Hikari. He noted that during my speech I had thanked my wife for sustaining us as a family and that I had thanked him too for performing the operation. Then he added:

I have been treating Hikari for twenty years, but I can't say that I really understand the full extent of Oe's feelings for his son. Still, in reading a number of his novels and critical works, I've gradually come to realize that what he experiences in his relationship with Hikari has a lot in common with the feelings of a doctor for his patients. Oe, his wife, and Hikari are all to be congratulated, in the warmest way.

It is, quite simply, one of the greatest pleasures of my life to have received such comments on my work from this doctor. Unfortunately, the year after he wrote it he fell ill. When I heard he had been hospitalized, I hurried off to see him without even checking to see whether he could have visitors. His diary entry for that day was the last one sent by Mrs. Moriyasu.

Oe came to see me here in the hospital. He arrived with Dr. Sugawara and seemed quite concerned about my health. He said that Hikari would be delighted to know I was doing well, and I told him I would be convalescing through June and would check up on Hikari by phone after that. He seemed relieved and left after giving me a copy of his latest book. . . . I'll have to have a look at it when I'm on vacation this summer.

His visit made me realize that there are still patients who need me, and it makes me anxious to get back to treating them. I still have a sense of myself as a doctor people depend on—I suppose over the years such feelings just take hold. I only hope that I can continue to improve, to polish my skills.

Dr. Moriyasu was the very epitome of the word "scrupulous." With me his manner was formal to the point of seeming at times almost brusque; in fact, it wasn't until after his death, when I saw the diary entries, that I realized his concern for the son had extended to the father as well. But on our regular visits to his office, he always had a ready joke for Hikari (who himself has a humorous side to him and is well aware of its effect on people). The boy brought out an elegant and utterly natural sense of humor in him.

I remember one rare occasion, though, when his manner even with me was a lot milder than usual. He was talking about his daughter, who had begun her medical studies and was interested in specializing in dermatology. (This was on the even rarer occasion of his asking a favor of me: he wanted me to give a talk from a novelist's perspective for her department at the university.) I remember especially how his face glowed with excitement, as if he himself were a young specialist, when he explained that in dermatology one was on the cutting edge of medical research. And mentally I filed away this other aspect of him—the scholarly one—along with the scrupulous humor I already knew.

From the patient's point of view, or that of the patient's family, it was reassuring to know that one could rely on his knowledge and skill as a brain surgeon, but the thing that gave us the most encouragement on a daily basis was this special character of his; and I can hardly imagine how lost we would have felt had he suddenly stopped being himself, even if his medical skills had remained unchanged. . . .

# Perfect Timing

"Does the World Remember Hiroshima?," broadcast on August 3 this year, was a project I had been working on for some time with my friends at NHK (the Japan Broadcasting Corporation). I am not, I should say, particularly experienced in television work, but there were reasons for my agreeing to be closely involved in this particular program, which was to commemorate the forty-fifth anniversary of the atomic bombings.

Ever since the year Hikari was born, I have found myself

returning again and again to Hiroshima. Hikari had his twenty-seventh birthday in June, so it is that many years from the time Hiroshima first assumed a central place in my work and became a way for me to think about our society, our world—about what it means to be human. I began with a book called *Hiroshima Notes*, and I have continued to address the topic on various occasions and in various forms. But if I were asked to sum up my thoughts one more time, I would say something to the following effect. It seems to me no exaggeration to suggest that what the citizens of those two cities experienced in the nuclear attack was the greatest misery suffered by human beings in the twentieth century. Moreover, though it is now nearly half a century since the "authority" of nuclear weapons assumed a central position in world affairs, the reality of this suffering can be seen to this day in the cataract-clouded eyes of the now elderly victims, in the deformities and handicaps suffered by their children, in elevated levels of cancer throughout the region, and in the other lingering effects of radiation.

There is, of course, no way ever to undo this disaster, but I want to focus for a moment on the efforts of those who, almost immediately after the bombs were dropped, began trying to bring relief to the victims and who, in a variety of different ways, continue those efforts to this very day. This summer, for example, I met an elderly woman who, as a new bride of seventeen with a husband away at the war, became a victim of the bomb at Hiroshima. She managed to survive both the excruciating pain of her burns and, later, rejection by her husband's family, and having brought up her children to be decent human beings, has now taken on the role of the "voice of Hiroshima," traveling the country to bring word of the horrors she experienced to a younger generation. This is someone who has seen firsthand both the "authority" of these weapons and the misery they inflict; but, far from losing heart, she has gone on doing what she can to repair the damage of that fateful summer day in 1945.

When I think of such people, however, the name that immediately comes to mind is that of Dr. Fumio Shigeto, director of the Atomic Bomb Hospital in Hiroshima. Forty-five years ago, Dr. Shigeto had just taken up his post as assistant director of the Red Cross Hospital there when the bomb was dropped. That morning, at the crucial hour, he was on his way to work, boarding a streetcar in front of Hiroshima Station; by the afternoon, he was confronted with the task of caring for untold numbers of injured people.

It has always struck me as ironic that his specialty at medical school had been radiology. This presumably was why he noticed at quite an early stage that the X-ray plates stored in the basement of the Red Cross Hospital had been exposed, which led him to conduct a careful study of both the victims' injuries and the physical damage to the city in terms of relation to ground zero. He was, then, one of the first to realize the true nature of these new weapons.

My first meeting with Dr. Shigeto was in August 1963, two months after Hikari was born. As a young father whose first child was deformed—a problem I still had no idea how to cope with—I'd gone off to write about the World Conference Against Atomic and Hydrogen Bombs in something of a daze. That particular year, the conference was in serious danger of breaking up over a dispute concerning whether Soviet Russia's nuclear armaments should be recognized as a means of "justifiable defense," and therefore as "instruments of peace." For me, however, the bigger question was: what had led me, at such a dire moment and in my nearly complete ignorance of the complexities of a large-scale political movement, to accept such an assignment in the first place?

There are only two factors I recall clearly that might have answered that question: one was the intense feeling that the problem of my child would end up suffocating me if I couldn't get out into a larger arena, see things from a broader perspective; and the other was the way I'd been moved by the utterly dejected manner of a young magazine editor after a visit to persuade me to do this piece for him. I remember watching him from the window of the second-floor apartment we were renting and thinking that I'd rarely seen anything as sad as that stooped figure. The young man, who later became a close friend as well as head of the Iwanami publishing company, had managed to get me to accept the assignment, but it seemed he wasn't at all happy about the idea of trying to draw a young novelist out of his funk over his sick child by sending him off to Hiroshima to write reportage. The feeling was connected, no doubt, with the fact that the man was himself still mourning the loss of his first child. . . .

The conference, with all its turbulent debate, was exhausting; but I did manage to fit in a visit to the Atomic Bomb Hospital, and as I listened to Dr. Shigeto talk about his own experiences as a bomb victim and about treating other cases, I found myself somehow profoundly consoled and encouraged, as if I were being cured of a serious illness. It is no exaggeration to say that in the course of that one conversation a whole new horizon was opened to me.

One of my teachers at university, Professor Kazuo Watanabe, a specialist in the French Renaissance, had, by way of introducing his favorite subject, offered us a number of definitions of the term "humanism," which he considered to be the core concept of the period. Among them was a simple axiom: "Neither too much hope nor too much despair"; and it was this line I recalled as I listened to the way Dr. Shigeto spoke of Hiroshima immediately after the bombing and of the task of treating the victims. Without too much hope or too much despair, he had simply dealt with the suffering as best he could. As I mentioned, it has always struck me as an odd coincidence that he should have arrived at his post in Hiroshima just at the moment he did, equipped with a specialized knowledge of radiology that allowed him to understand what he was up against. But it is perhaps no less strange that I should have set out for the same city at the moment of the first and greatest crisis of my life, and there had the chance to talk to this same doctor. Moreover, I, too, came equipped with the means to understand the significance of what he was saying: namely, Watanabe's definition of humanism.

These vital moments, when various disparate elements come together at exactly the right time and place, as if by fate, are in practice simply a part of life's natural process. By now, with the benefit of so much more experience, I no longer doubt this. But there have been times when such moments have seemed like signs of something else: examples—albeit rather flashy ones—of some supreme being's perfect timing; a sort of cosmic double play.

2

Dr. Shigeto's home was a substantial old house surrounded by luxuriant foliage in a neighborhood of similar houses on the outskirts of a saké-brewing town not far from Hiroshima. Though the doctor had said that he was the son of peasants, the prominent position they occupied, even in an area of prosperous tradition like that, became all the more evident when, on paying him a visit there, I took a walk with him and his wife in the town's ancient cemetery. As we wandered along a green mountain path, his wife, still vigorous despite her age, told me of her memories of the days after the bomb.

Even in the outlying villages, she said, they had learned almost immediately that a powerful bomb had been dropped on Hiroshima and that the damage was tremendous. Then, the badly wounded had begun arriving. By evening, she had all but given up hope that her husband could have survived, and was making plans to go into the city the next day to search for his body. She was on her way to buy her train ticket when she met her husband. It seems he had taken refuge at the house of a friend who had a brewery and, having toasted his survival a few times too many, had decided it would be dangerous to ride his bicycle home and was forced to push it most of the way, except for a stretch where he was given a lift in a truck.

Apparently, since the center of the city was declared off-limits, he had begun trying to treat the wounded at a parade ground on the outskirts of town where many of them had taken shelter. In those first few hours there was, of course, no real treatment for the injuries inflicted by the mysterious bomb, but even if he could do nothing but dress the burns with oil, the fact that a doctor was doing the dressing must have been a comfort to them. He remembered at one stage noticing a soldier, wounded like everyone else, standing near-by saluting him. When he asked why he was doing this, the man said it was his way of thanking a civilian doctor for helping the victims of this war that he and his kind had brought upon them. . . . By the time he finally made his way home, though, he was too tired presumably to tell his wife about episodes like this. And yet, the following day, he again set out for Hiroshima, this time remaining for several weeks, unable to leave his work at the Red Cross Hospital. Eventually, at the end of a month, he arrived home utterly exhausted.

At this point in her story, I managed to ask his wife a question I'd been wanting to ask Dr. Shigeto since we first met: did the doctor himself have any symptoms of radiation sickness? She smiled as she told me that until his exposure to the bomb he had been rather frail and high-strung, but since then he'd been more relaxed and far more robust. From this rather curious fact I could only conclude that, for Dr. Shigeto, who had just been entering middle age in 1945, those years spent caring for victims of radiation and running the hospital had somehow served to revitalize him physically and emotionally, preparing him for renewed activity. It was only later that I was able to put a name to this renewal when I read about what Erik Erikson calls the "mid-life identity crisis." As I see it, having confronted the disaster of Hiroshima, the doctor was able to overcome his own identity crisis and move on with his life, thus bringing comfort and hope to countless other people.

There is, I suppose, a personal reason why I am given to this sort of speculation: I experienced an identity crisis of my own at the age of twenty-eight, in the year Hikari was born. I had begun my career as a writer rather early, but in many of the ways that matter, I had been slow to mature. Thus, though the experts would no doubt find my use of Erikson's terminology rather loose, I like to think of what I was experiencing at that time as the "identity crisis of my youth." It was in the midst of this crisis that my son's birth burst like a bombshell; and it was through the pain of this experience that I somehow regained my equilibrium. My son was operated on and welcomed home, and in the act of fictionalizing those events in the form of a novel, I was finally able to synthesize them, to make some kind of sense out of a senseless situation. In a strange way, Hikari's birth, too, was a case of "perfect timing," an immensely important event that occurred at a vital moment in my life.


3

Dr. Shigeto often mentioned a young ophthalmologist

whose story, he said, was among his saddest memories. The
Red Cross Hospital that summer had been overflowing with
the injured, while the bodies of the dead lay in piles in the
courtyard where a fire burned all day long to cremate them.
In the midst of the horror, this young doctor had come to
Shigeto. What could they do in the face of such an unspeak-
able tragedy, he wanted to know. The human race, he said,
was bound to end like this, the whole feeble species dying in
utter misery; but for those who were left behind, there didn't
seem to be a sane way to go on living. If they were honest
with themselves, it was useless to continue treating the crowds
of people dying before their very eyes when there was virtually nothing anyone *could* do for them.

Faced with this outburst, Dr. Shigeto had answered that
they had no choice but to try to help as many as they could,
one patient at a time. Soon afterward, however, he'd found
the young doctor in the corridor, hanging from one of the
beams exposed by the bomb. Shigeto finished this story, told
with an unmistakable bitterness in his voice, by gesturing
toward a wall in the hospital (still preserved today) that bris-
tles with glass shards driven into it by the force of the explo-
sion.

I am told that Dr. Shigeto also offered him some gentler
advice, urging him to leave that city of rubble and go for a
rest just over the hills where the fields and forests were still
green. Not long ago, I went to visit the graves of Dr. Shigeto
and his wife, and saw for myself again the bright colors of
the surrounding scenery; and when I imagine the doctor
reminding his young colleague that it was still green "just

over the hills," I like to think that I know what was in his heart, what memories he took with him when he returned to Hiroshima that day, of the lingering green of his family home and the wife and children he left there.

Many of the people I have met in Hiroshima over the years are dead now. It is safe to say that only the rare individual has lived to a relatively healthy old age. In particular, of those I got to know after they'd been admitted to the Atomic Bomb Hospital, not a single one was ever able to go back to leading a normal life. At one point Dr. Shigeto told me that foreign visitors to the hospital who occasionally returned for a second visit invariably asked to see the patients they'd met in the past; but as pleasant as the idea of such reunions might have been, none was ever possible.

# Compassion

IT TAKES A CERTAIN amount of courage—a sad kind of courage, perhaps—to admit that there have been (and in fact still are) moments when we as a family (and I in particular) have been unable to control our anger with Hikari. It is an anger that I imagine isn't unlike that felt on occasion by doctors and nurses toward their patients, or by physio- and psychotherapists toward theirs—a realization that conjures up for me an image of myself, on a day in the not too distant future, as a crotchety old patient making trouble for my family and helpers and being treated accordingly by them.

I think back to an incident that occurred when Hikari was about five or six years old. At the time he was larger and heavier than the average child of his age, but his mental development was perhaps no more than that of a three-year-old. When we took him out for walks, he would choose the most inopportune time and place to collapse in a heap or rush off in whatever direction caught his fancy, nearly dislocating the shoulder of the person holding his hand. On the day in question, I had set out with Hikari for a department store in Shibuya. In retrospect, I suppose the excursion may have been the result of some minor argument with my wife, which might explain why it was just the two of us. At any rate, the department store where we went to do our shopping consisted of an old and a newer building, connected on one of the upper floors by a passage; and it was while we were making our way through the sports section in the old building that Hikari decided to make yet another of his frequent, forceful changes in direction. Though the shock was enough to draw a groan from me, I managed to keep my composure and explain to him that we were going where I said we were going. Still, Hikari continued to pull, determined to follow his own instincts.

I can remember even now the strange sense of disembodiment I felt at that moment, as if I were being plucked right out of reality itself, which I assume is one of the side effects of sudden anger. In any case, for some reason I simply let go of Hikari's hand and went straight to the new building to do the shopping I'd come to do. Then I spent a few minutes looking over the latest offerings in the book section. Finally,

I made my way back to where I had left him, but naturally there was no sign of the boy. It was only then that I panicked. I ran off to report a lost child, and almost immediately the loudspeaker began broadcasting his name and description; but I knew that even if he did hear the announcement, Hikari would either have no idea that he was lost or no way of doing anything about it. I started to search the floor where I'd left him in both the old and new buildings; then I searched the floors above and below. I had wandered through the store for nearly two hours when I stopped to rest on the landing of the staircase in the new building. It was while I was thinking about the call I would have to make to my wife, staring vacantly out the foggy window, that I spotted him: a short, oddly bent figure, not unlike a dog, making its way slowly but steadily up the stairs of the old building. I dashed to the floor with the connecting passage, and on my way down the opposite side I found him, scrambling along in his overalls, red wool cap pulled down around his ears. His pudgy cheeks were flushed from the exertion, but otherwise his face betrayed no unusual emotion. He barely glanced in my direction. Still, that afternoon as we rode home on the train he held tight to my hand.

Since that day I have often imagined the frightening consequences we might have had to face: we might simply have lost him for good, or he could have fallen down the stairs, or had his hands crushed as he tried to crawl onto an escalator. Would I ever have been able to see myself as anything other than a criminally negligent father who had sent his son toddling off to his fate? In all likelihood, this one momentary lapse would have meant the end of my life with my family. And even now, because of this experience, whenever I see an article of the sort that appears frequently in the newspapers these days about some young mother dropping her baby on the floor to stop it crying, I can never bring myself to condemn these inexperienced, unfortunate people; instead, I identify with them, imagine myself in their shoes, feel their torment. I have no doubt that there are instinctive emotions that allow us to raise our children lovingly and well; but there is also instinct involved in that sudden, inexplicable anger one can feel toward a baby crying in the night. . . .

Knowing this, I am all the more amazed at my wife's unwavering devotion to Hikari. Throughout his life, she has been the very image of patience. Still, even she occasionally gets angry with him, and at such times someone else in the family, myself or one of our other children, generally steps in to take the role of his defender. Recently, however, I've noticed that we don't all play the part in quite the same way. While my younger son and I tend simply to support Hikari regardless of the circumstances, my daughter first gathers all the facts in the case and then explains them to him, often urging him to reconsider his position. In the end, I suppose, she proves to be his best ally.

2

Lately, Hikari and I have fallen out over something rather different from the relatively innocent arm-wrenching of his youth. It happens that someone in the family has to take Hikari to his vocational training center each morning and pick him up in the afternoon. More often than not, my younger son and daughter get this chore to do, but on the rare occasions when I have made the trip with him, it hasn't gone particularly smoothly, a fact that has become something of a sore point between us (though as I write this I can hear how absurd it sounds).

From time to time, in fact, I am recruited to go and pick up Hikari just as I have settled down with a book or set to work on a manuscript. This interruption is complicated, moreover, by the fact that I don't drive and we don't own a car. Indeed, my wife is the only one of us with a driver's license, but she got it so long ago she would probably have to brush up on her driving skills were we to consider getting a car for taking Hikari to and fro. Anyway, at present, the bus and train ride to the center and back takes a full hour and a half, which gives me plenty of time to grumble to myself about how I would rather be at home doing whatever I was doing before.

There are, in any case, two crosswalks that have to be negotiated on the way from the training center to the station, and one in particular is at a wide main road where it seems you wait forever, while the trucks and cars whiz by, for the crossing light to turn green. Now I knew that Hikari would have been terrified if the light had turned red while he was in the middle of the intersection, and there was always the danger that he might have a seizure or some other problem while crossing, so I'd made a point of repeatedly warning him that if he ever had to go to the center by himself he should be particularly careful at this intersection. In fact, though, I knew that the warning wasn't strictly necessary since Hikari is exceedingly conscientious about things like that and obeys traffic lights with something approaching religious fervor. One day, however, as I was hurrying him toward the station, we came to this intersection while the crossing light was green. I could see that the people who had been waiting for the light were already more than halfway across, but I grabbed Hikari's arm and set off at a trot. Though the signal did start to flash while we were still in the street, we made it to the other side with time to spare. However, when I turned to congratulate Hikari on our little success and to compliment him on his brisk pace, there was no reply. He just wrenched free of my grip and turned to glare at the signal, his arms akimbo like the guardian demons at a temple gate. The rest of the way home, he followed in silence a few steps behind.

In the meantime, childish as it may sound, I got angry too. I didn't speak to him on the bus and continued to ignore him when I went back to my work and he sprawled out on the living room floor to listen to some music. For his part, Hikari seemed convinced of the justice of his indignation directed at a father who had been unwilling to wait prudently for the next light, had found it necessary to rush him along at an unaccustomed pace, and, worst of all, had subjected him to the terror of the changing signal. Still, while he seemed to have no intention of compromising, he did appear concerned about his father's gloomy silence and began, almost immediately, to look for ways to make a peace offering without sacrificing his pride. When the phone rang he answered it with unusual promptness and, waving off my wife's attempts to take it from him, brought me the receiver after announcing who it was with uncustomary precision. Next, he brought me the evening paper. Then, when one of my friends made an appearance in some television program, he watched carefully to see if I had noticed. Rightly enough, though, he gave no sign that he was prepared to apologize for sulking about the crossing incident. It wasn't long, however, before I was overcome with shame at the way I'd been acting and began looking for my own ways of making up—though without damaging my own parental dignity. . . . I can imagine how hard it must have been for the rest of the family not to laugh out loud at our little comedy.

### 3

To my mind, the poet Shiki Masaoka is one of the few people who has ever been able to write honestly and accurately about the feelings that develop between a sick or handicapped person and the family taking care of him, and do so in a manner that has a universal bearing. As a boy from Ehime prefecture (on the southern island of Shikoku which was also Shiki's home), I was familiar with this late nineteenth-century poet from quite an early age. But it wasn't only his poetry that interested me; I was also fascinated by the fact that Shiki, who spent years confined to a sickbed, had seen fit to record his irritation with the quality of his sister's care and to give his opinions on everything from nursing to women's education.

There are undoubtedly a number of troubling points in the behavior of this poet who accomplished so much of his most important work while a virtual invalid. His relationship with his neighbor and patron Katsunan Kuga, for example, was sometimes less than admirable. Kuga, it seems, used to dress up his young daughter in a beautiful kimono and bring her to visit Shiki, to cheer him up, without Shiki apparently giving any thought to the danger of infection from his tuberculosis. Likewise, Shiki's relationship with his mother and sister, who cared for him devotedly to the very end, is problematic. But perhaps most disturbing of all are the complaints he has to make about his sister Ritsu in his final diary, "Random Thoughts While Lying Flat on My Back."

> Ritsu is a stern, pragmatic woman, as cold and unfeeling as a stone. She nurses me out of a sense of duty, but she offers no compassion or comfort. She will do anything I ask of her directly, but refuses to understand when I hint at my needs. From time to time I expound to her on the subject of compassion and fellow feeling yet it seems to fall on deaf ears, for there is no explaining a feeling to one who lacks any such thing. Unfortunate as it is, this leaves me little choice but to abandon the attempt. . . .

More petulantly, he writes:

> At times she seems to be utterly indifferent to my

wishes, even when I express them quite openly by saying, for example, that I would dearly like some dumplings. A person of any consideration, hearing that an invalid wanted to eat a particular kind of food, would immediately go out to buy it, but not Ritsu, who has never once done anything of the sort. Thus I am forced to give direct orders: "Go and get me some dumplings." When told to do something explicitly, at least, she never refuses.

As a definition of Shiki's "compassion," I would propose something to the effect of "an active yet almost automatic ability to enter into the feelings of another person." This comes very close to "imagination," reminding me of what Rousseau says in *Emile* on the subject of education: that "only the imagination can teach us another's pain." So, despite the subjective tone of his comments on his sister's style of nursing (which one assumes were influenced by his concern over her failed marriage and rather independent character), the point he is making is nevertheless a fundamental one.

He was also writing an essay as he was keeping this diary, and in it he wonders aloud whether there might be some way of instilling in Japanese women the kind of spontaneous compassion that would allow them to nurse people as he would have them do it, or, as Rousseau would put it, a way to get them to "imagine" other people's suffering. The argument he makes follows a "logical" pattern until he reaches a point where he seems to feel a certain embarrassment at what he must, from the beginning, have known to be an unjust sentiment, the venting of an invalid's anger and frustration; for he comes out in favor generally of women's education, seeing it as necessary anyway. And indeed, after nursing him to the end of his long illness, Ritsu completed her education, becoming a teacher and, though she never had a family of her own, living a productive, independent life. Thus his essay, which he probably had no reason to think she would read when it was published in a newspaper, can be seen as his admittedly obscure attempt at an apology. I like to think that in later years, when time had provided sufficient distance, she became one of his more understanding and sympathetic readers—and if I am right in supposing this, one can imagine her satisfaction at being reconciled with her dead brother.

I find, however, that these notions of "active compassion" and the exercise of the imagination take on a special meaning in the case of mentally handicapped children and the families, doctors, nurses, and therapists who look after them. How, practically speaking, can these "patients" communicate their needs and wants when they don't fully understand them themselves? Hikari, for example, particularly when he was younger, never expressed a desire for anything, not even something as simple as Shiki's dumplings. And realizing this only increases my admiration for my wife's patience and compassion in the task of imagining his needs—above all, his need for music.

To a certain extent, Shiki was probably reveling in the gloom and boredom of his sickroom; yet I also feel he tried to dispel that atmosphere and generally raise his spirits, using not only his diary but sketches of flowers to do so. I sometimes wonder what his mother and sister must have felt when they saw those sketches. For many years now, while she was raising Hikari, my wife, too, has been drawing plants and flowers, and although they may not be the equal of Shiki's in a purely artistic sense, whenever I sit down to look through her sketchbooks my head is filled with thoughts of the complicated ties that bind a sick person and his family together, the sufferer and his comforter.

# *Acceptance*

IT IS QUITE some time since I first came across the term "rehabilitation," which in Japanese is a borrowed word. In fact, it was in the form of *réhabilitation* that I was introduced to it, in one of the French novels I always seemed to be reading as a student. I remember that it was used in the sense of preparing a former prisoner to return to ordinary society and there reestablish his reputation, but I have no idea now what the book in question was. I'd like to think it was something impressive, a novel by Balzac perhaps, which would do credit to my image of myself as a twenty-two-year-old, but it is just as likely to

have been a detective story by Simenon or some other popular writer. Be that as it may, I am struck by the fact that one
only has to substitute the sick person confined to a hospital
for the criminal confined to a prison to get something close
to current medical use of the term "rehabilitation," meaning
the physical and social training that aims at restoring a sick
or disabled person to his or her normal life.

I had my first concrete experience with this branch of
medicine (which, I learned recently, was developed around
the end of World War II, chiefly in America) when I received
a letter from Satoshi Ueda of the Department of Rehabilitative
Medicine at Tokyo University Hospital inviting me to speak
at an international conference on rehabilitation to be held in
Tokyo in 1988. As I read the pamphlet enclosed with the letter explaining the nature of the conference, my interest was
aroused. I was particularly impressed that this new field of
medicine was concerned with treating a patient's physical
and emotional difficulties as a single phenomenon. Still, I
wasn't sure that I had anything useful to say to such a gath-
ering, so I suggested he contact someone more appropriate.

When Dr. Ueda wrote back, asking me to reconsider, he
included a copy of his book called *Thoughts on Rehabilitation:
Restoring the Disabled to Full Humanity*, and this I found
deeply instructive. Systematically and precisely, the author
exposes the emotional stages experienced by a person who
becomes disabled. How, he asks, does someone make the
painful psychological adjustments to his disability, come to
accept himself in his new condition, and learn to function in
his family and in society at large? Reading further, I began

to see a certain analogy between the process of rehabilitation, which leads the disabled person to a state of acceptance of his disability, and a literary—or, perhaps, cultural—theory which might be said to lead to an acceptance of one's condition in life. And though I still wasn't sure that what I had to say would be worthwhile, by the time I'd finished the book I was determined to give the speech. The following excerpts should help to explain, as honestly as I can, why I, a novelist, had the presumption to address an audience of international experts in this field.

> Twenty-five years ago, my first son was born with brain damage. This was a blow, to say the least; and yet, as a writer, I must acknowledge the fact that the central theme of my work, throughout much of my career, has been the way my family has managed to live with this handicapped child. Indeed, I would have to admit that the very ideas that I hold about this society and the world at large—my thoughts, even, about whatever there might be that transcends our limited reality—are based on and learned through living with him.

I went on to say that the thing I'd wanted and searched for most keenly in my life with Hikari, before he was even able to speak, was a way of knowing what was going on in his heart. And then one day the paths of communication were opened by a wild bird's call, a sound my son was always drawn to, and that process, too, found its way into a novel. . . .

Essentially, in writing a novel about a handicapped child

one is building a model of what it means to be handicapped, making it as complete and comprehensive as possible yet also concrete and personal. Nor is the model confined to the handicapped person alone, but something that encompasses the people around him and, by extension, the world we live in.

I then spoke about the way the model-building I was doing in my novels overlapped with what Dr. Ueda had done for the developmental process by which a person who has suffered a disabling illness or injury comes finally to accept his or her handicap. He divides up the stages in the process this way:

> When a person suffers an accident or illness that results in a disability, he initially enters what might be called a "shock phase," characterized by apathy and withdrawal. This is followed by the "denial phase," a psychological defense mechanism in which the illness or injury is simply blocked. Eventually, when the realization is made that the disability is permanent and can never be reversed, the patient enters the "confusion phase," in which anger and resentment are typical, as well as grief and depression. However, the goal is for the disabled person to recognize his personal responsibility for his life and emerge from dependency, a process that is accomplished during the "effort phase" in which a solution is sought. Having passed through each of these stages, the disabled person ultimately reaches the "acceptance phase," in which he has adjusted to the idea of his handicap as a

part of his identity and is able to resume his role in his family or society.

To which I added my own version of this process:

> In trying to portray my son in the literary model known as a novel, I have passed through five similar stages. In the case of a person like him, with a mental disability, it isn't the individual himself but rather his family that has to pass from the "shock phase" to the "acceptance phase." In a sense, my work on this theme has mirrored that process. I have had to learn through concrete experience to answer such questions as how a handicapped person and his family can survive the shock, denial, and confusion phases and learn to live with each of those particular kinds of pain. I then had to find out how we could move beyond this to a more positive adjustment, before finally reaching our own "acceptance phase"— in effect coming to accept ourselves as handicapped, as the family of a handicapped person. And it was only then that I felt the development of my work itself was at last complete.

## 2

The *Concise Oxford English Dictionary* defines "acceptance" as "consent to receive," "receiving gladly"; to which it adds synonyms such as "approval," "trust," and "tolerance." This range of meanings interests me in that it seems to situate the etymology of the word in terms of Western religious values that stress the need to trust and acknowledge and coexist with other people despite difficult circumstances.

Last year, on World Disabled Persons Day, NHK broadcast a number of programs having to do with the handicapped. I was asked to serve as a commentator for these programs, despite the fact that I am merely the father of one disabled person and unqualified to offer expert opinions or advice. Still, I jumped at the chance because it meant that I would hear real experts on the subject and get to see the special films that had been produced for the occasion which, through negligence and a certain cowardice, I might otherwise never watch; in other words, I would educate myself a bit.

The films, in particular, were of an extremely high quality. In them one could see the essence of what "acceptance" means for the handicapped, expressed in a way that clearly and richly illuminated the dictionary definition of the word, but also, beyond that, provided a specific vision of a very human way of living. Among the films was a wonderful documentary recording one portion of a trip that a twenty-year-old woman made alone in a wheelchair. From her home to Kyoto, and from there to her grandmother's house in the country, the camera followed this young woman as she confronted various new experiences and grew stronger from them. At the same time, however, the rather beautiful but determined expression on her face showed traces of the suffering and sense of futility that the journey must have entailed. Though I haven't got her permission to quote her exactly, something she said impressed me deeply and I would like to give the gist of it here: she said that she felt it was important for disabled people to go out and do what they wanted to do, even if it meant inconveniencing others. They might have to ask someone able-bodied for help, and that might not always go down too well, but it didn't matter as long as they were doing what their heart was telling them to do.

This comment reminded me of something that happened at the same lake in North Karuizawa where Hikari had once identified a water rail. I had taken him out for an hour's row on the lake, and we had made our way back to the little marina and were about to climb onto the pier when we ran into some trouble. Hikari had stood up to get out of the boat, but when it started to rock he became frightened and froze in a crouch. As I sat trying to stabilize the boat, I called encouragement to him, but all he could manage to do was slowly pivot his feet back and forth, creeping ever so gradually in the direction of the pier. To my dismay, it was in the middle of this interminable process that one of the two dock attendants who were holding the boat —a large, handsome youth—suddenly just wandered off toward the boathouse. The boat began to rock violently, and I had to leap onto the dock to help the other person get Hikari safely ashore.

I was also reminded of a situation encountered by my daughter, who had obviously had considerable experience working with the handicapped at home but nevertheless decided to volunteer for similar activities while in college. One of the people she was helping, an elderly woman, called our house on a regular basis to ask for assistance in getting to the hospital or elsewhere. Sometimes these calls came on days other than the ones on which my daughter was free to help, and if she had a test to take or a paper due, she would stand by the phone, receiver in hand, looking lost and bothered. When this happened, though, she made it clear that she didn't want any advice from me. In fact, she kept everything to do with her volunteer work very much to herself, and if she caught any hint of my wanting to write about some of the people she met in this way, she would walk around with a look of protest on her face, refusing to let up until I abandoned the idea.

The truth is that I, too, felt this was more than just a college club activity, that it was a genuine social service and as such required her to respect the wishes of those she was helping more than her own, but I used to heave a sigh of relief from my vantage point on the couch near the phone when, after a long conversation, she managed to persuade this particular woman that she couldn't come that day. This doesn't prevent me, nevertheless, from hoping my daughter will learn the willing acceptance of inconveniences that the girl in the wheelchair spoke about (though, incidentally, I remember one scene in the film showing her struggling uphill to see some temple in Kyoto, refusing to be pushed even when the cameraman and producer were there to help). . . .

In another scene, the young woman was telling a guest at an inn where she was staying about the car accident that had left her paralyzed from the waist down, and about the shock she'd felt at the time. Her tone was calm, almost cheerful, as she spoke of her early efforts to accept her life in a wheelchair. The movie also showed her persuading her parents to allow her to go on the trip and then phoning various hotels to make reservations, a process that was complicated by the fact that she was traveling alone and in a wheelchair. But for every innkeeper who refused her quite bluntly, there was another who carefully explained the layout of the inn and how it would be possible for her to get to her room.

Listening to these exchanges—and my daughter also spent days calling various cheap inns for an outing of her group of disabled people—gave me a real taste of the way the handicapped are treated in Japan today. It takes a certain strength to change things for the better, but both sides—the girl in the wheelchair and the volunteer, my daughter—demonstrated this as they laid out their conditions and persisted in their negotiations, probably without much expectation of a warm response.

At the end of the film, which is also the end of this journey of hardship and strong emotions, the young woman at last makes her way to her grandmother's house in the country. As she waits in the pleasant old entranceway, her face reveals her anxiety at their first meeting since her accident but also a certain pride in her accomplishment, her solo trip, which she can't wait to talk about. Her grandmother appears, crawling along as fast as she can, her kimono barely tied in her haste to see the girl, and there follows a touching yet almost wordless reunion. The blood ties between these two women—one in a wheelchair, the other having lost the use of her legs in old age—are plain to see in their dignified, rather stubborn bearing and a certain frankness that comes from a good upbringing.

Soon afterward, the two are facing each other over the *kotatsu*, still saying very little. The old woman seems to be a bit senile and finds it hard to string words together; the family treats her rather like an elderly child, and her daughter-in-law tends to insert comments tactfully covering her silences, moving the conversation along. (I was reminded of my own mother-in-law, whose speech is often "dubbed in" by other people.) Eventually, we learn that the girl has brought a charm for her grandmother from a temple in Kyoto, and as we watch the latter anxiously unwrapping the gift and expressing her delight, we come to realize that this is a person who has learned to "accept" the debility of old age. She sits, smiling and silent, facing her young visitor who has had to accept her own handicap, with tears welling up in her eyes; and this acceptance, of the pain and disappointments they have each overcome, seems to illuminate both their faces.

It is probably safe to say that, had they both been well, they might not have achieved such a deep understanding together. It would have been quite natural for the grand-daughter, in the full blush of youth and health, to resent the inevitable decline of old age into which her grandmother was heading. But what we see in the film are two women, one young and the other old, each of whom has learned to put up with her situation; and in that shared experience they have discovered a certain sympathy, a gentle meeting of the minds that seems to envelop them in a light all their own— and impart to them a quality that merits genuine respect.

## 3

I ended my talk for the international conference on rehabilitation with the following words (at the risk, I realized, of
being seen as overly personal and emotional, especially perhaps by the foreign participants).

My greatest source of pride these days is the fact that
my brain-damaged son is a decent, tolerant, trust-
worthy human being who also happens to have a good
sense of humor. And I would add that his strength of
character has had no small influence on our family.

In the course of living with him, I have come to
know many disabled people, their families, and those
who help with their rehabilitation, and I have seen how
each shoulders his or her own burden. The signs of this
suffering are clearly visible on the faces of the handicapped, even when they have reached the stage of
acceptance; and those around them are no doubt simi-
larly marked. But I believe there is another sign that all
these people share: their common decency.

I used the English word "decency," a word that is especially
hard to translate because it embodies a range of meanings; but
as a possible equivalent I have in mind not a single word but
the atmosphere of the meeting between the young woman in
the film and her grandmother: the light I mentioned, which
seemed to surround them, and a certain quality of character
that provoked respect. It is this special aura they had that for
me is the very definition of the word "decency."

# "Let's Just Get on with It"

RECENTLY, we held a young people's concert, the second in fact, in the village where I was born (which has actually been swallowed up by a larger town). The inhabitants of that wooded valley were organizing various activities to help conserve the local environment, and the concert came about because it was something we in Tokyo could set up to offer our support.

This year, our friend the pianist Jun Toyama came with us for the trip and invited a number of his colleagues along, talented musicians who are active both as performers and teachers in Japan. The concert was scheduled just as the cherry trees were coming into flower, but the flight on which most of the musicians were due to arrive ran into a heavy rainstorm and was forced to turn back from Shikoku and land at Osaka. The young people organizing the event were a bit "disconcerted," to say the least. The audience, which included people who had come from a fair distance away, was still waiting for the performers to make their round-about way via Bullet Train and across the new Seto Bridge, so I filled in by giving a rather protracted speech, and Toyama, who had come down earlier with us, followed up with some solo piano pieces. Eventually the others arrived, and we had the scheduled trio, quartet, and solo flute performances. By the time the program was over, the audience had been in their seats for more than six hours, but hardly a soul left early.

Despite their long journey, the musicians had barely paused to put on their stage clothes before starting the performance. As they began to play, I was struck by the way those familiar faces seemed to change, taking on the characteristics peculiar to masters of their individual instruments, violin, cello, or flute. They seemed to embody a very human urge to make music, indeed to live through music, and I wondered whether my impression wasn't shared by the audience of more than five hundred (an enormous number for that part of the country).

For me, the concert was more than usually memorable because it included some of Hikari's compositions: solos for piano and flute and a work based on one of his tunes performed by a quartet. No doubt for the composer, sitting at my side, the experience was the memory of a lifetime. There have been moments recently when Hikari has seemed rather gloomy as he heads off for the training center—something that may be a function of his age. But the face that appeared for a moment on the local news that evening, that of the young composer receiving a bouquet of flowers after the concert, was the picture of joy and excitement.

2

This year we brought out a second collection of Hikari's compositions for flute and piano. In the afterword, I wrote:

Among Hikari's pleasures in life are going out for fast food with his sister and trying to guess the answers on TV quiz programs, but the better part of his free time is spent listening to classical music on the radio, on CDs, or on his old LPs. Beyond all this, however, is his composing—in which listening to music of course plays a role—and his music lessons, which together are the most important aspect, the center, of his life.

The way my son has structured his world puts me in mind of Maritain's definition of "habit." The French philosopher was referring to "artistic habit," but I doubt if it would violate the spirit of his thought to expand the meaning somewhat. It has always seemed to me that people build up the architecture of their profession or occupation over many years and on the basis of accumulated experience. This process is a product of the cooperation of every aspect of themselves, both conscious and unconscious. There is, in other words, something in the scientist that is difficult to separate from his research; likewise with the artisan, whose work, in a sense, is part of who he is. It is this fundamental element that Maritain identifies as the "habit" by which human beings live their lives.

Hikari's "life habit" is composition. Without exaggerating, one can say that music and the manner in which he creates it are for him, as someone whose mental development will always be that of a child, the principal way in which he can express himself. Equally, had he never taken up composing, my family and I would have remained forever ignorant of the delicate existence that was locked away deep inside him. But once given the means of expression—in his case, a way to construct melodies and harmonies—and encouraged to use them, he has produced things that, when brought to life by the piano and the flute, serve as his link with humanity.

In considering Jacques Maritain's notion of "habit" or "life habit," both with regard to Hikari and my own life and work, I am aware that my understanding of the idea has been helped considerably by exposure to the life and writings of the American novelist Flannery O'Connor. O'Connor read Maritain's work carefully and even carried on a correspondence with him while he was teaching at Princeton; and it seems that, perhaps based on this contact, consciously or unconsciously, she proceeded to construct for herself a "novelist's habit." It was her experience, she wrote, that when a work, perhaps by means she didn't herself understand, turned out to be a success—not in terms of its popularity but as a work of art—it was thanks to this habit that it did so. And I am sure it is the same accumulated practice that comes into play when the obstacles encountered by all those who labor in the fields of art are somehow—by trial and error—cleared to reveal a landscape no one has seen before.

Like her father before her, O'Connor suffered from lupus, which afflicted her in her early twenties when she was just beginning her writing career and killed her before her fortieth birthday. She produced her wonderful stories, then, as she struggled, stoically yet cheerfully, against a disease for which the only hope lay in the discovery of some new drug. The history of her inner development through this process can be glimpsed not only in those stories but in a final, brave, sympathetic letter written from her sickbed and included in her collected correspondence, which was published as *The Habit of Being*. (O'Connor, I would note, was born in the same year as Yukio Mishima, a writer whose attitude toward life and death couldn't have been more different from her own.)

The letter, scrawled almost illegibly as she lay dying and discovered by her mother after her death, was written to Maryat Lee, a playwright who was her lifelong friend. It concerns, of all things, some crank phone calls that had been worrying Lee at the time, and is full of kind and practical advice. O'Connor, in other words, was the sort of person who would concern herself with a friend's needs even in the last moments of her life. "Cowards," she wrote,

> can be just as vicious as those who declare themselves—more so. Don't take any romantic attitude toward that call. Be properly scared and go on doing what you have to do, but take the necessary precautions. And call the police. That might be a lead for them.
>
> Don't know when I'll send those stories. I've felt too bad to type them.

Sally Fitzgerald, another old friend of hers and the editor of her collected letters, writes that O'Connor had, in addition to her artistic "habit" as a novelist, something else:

> . . . [I]n the course of living in accordance with her formative beliefs, as she consciously and profoundly wished to do, she acquired as well, I think, a second distinguished habit, which I have called "the habit of being": an excellence not only of action but of interior disposition and activity that increasingly reflected the object, the being, which specified it, and was itself reflected in what she did and said.

This quality Ms. Fitzgerald refers to was perhaps nowhere more evident, in her correspondence, than in this last letter of hers.

3

In the course of taking Hikari to the training center or

picking him up in the evening, I have encountered a number of the parents—particularly the mothers—of handicapped children, and on their faces and in their behavior I have recognized the unmistakable signs of hardship. Over the years a number of these people have disappeared, one taken by cancer, another because she was forced to put her child in an institution, some having simply been overwhelmed by the burden of making the daily trip there; but in spite of the fact that we rarely spoke, I can still remember each of them, along with their children, in all their individuality. If I were pressed to say what it is that they all shared, it would be the sense that every one of them, at some decisive moment, had said to themselves: "We've got no choice. Let's just get on with it." And they were still doing so.

It is sentimental, however, and inaccurate as well to think that the lives of the mothers of handicapped children are just a constant struggle. The truth is that their children give them real joy—a joy that I've overheard, for example, in the conversations between these mothers, and sometimes grandmothers, while waiting for the bus to return from a field trip, or seen on their faces when at last the bus arrives and they're reunited with their excited kids. I can attest to it, too, from my own experience at home. And yet I also know that both my wife and I have said to ourselves on any number of occasions those too familiar words: "We've got no choice. Let's just get on with it."

There is another thought, however, that occurs perhaps even more frequently: namely, that the handicapped children themselves, more often than not, put up with their pains and trials without complaint and go about the task of living their lives with much the same attitude of "getting on with it." I can remember once having to give Hikari a long-distance scolding while I was away teaching at the University of California at Berkeley. My wife had put him on the phone after asking me to speak to him about some act of disobedience; and about ten days after the call, I received a letter from him: "It's no good," he wrote. "I should never have lived to be twenty." But, though he may have felt that way at times, he has never acted on those feelings, never just given up and stayed all day in bed. And this, surely—the fact that he actually gets up every morning looking forward to seeing his friends at the training center, that he takes a certain pleasure in the contents of his lunch box, that he comes home and listens to records or throws himself into his composing—all this is evidence of his own basic resolution to "just get on with it." And it is true to say that this resolution has been one of the cornerstones of our family life.

4

One of my books, *Rouze Up O Young Men of the New Age!*, was written at a period in my life when I was absorbed in the works of William Blake. The title of this series of short stories about Hikari is a line from the preface of one of the long poems that Blake called "prophecies," a word he used in a rather idiosyncratic sense.

Blake, whose life spanned a period of tremendous upheaval in Europe from the mid-eighteenth to the mid-nineteenth centuries, evolved an utterly original vision of the world in his mysteriously beautiful poems and prints, at the heart of which were two preoccupations. One was his engagement in the crucial historical events of his period, namely American independence and the French Revolution. As proof of this involvement, he left behind a print of the American Declaration of Independence, inscribed within a design incorporating various Christian iconography, and a poem that salutes the French Revolution as a "sign" of the liberation of mankind. He even spoke publicly of his hope that Napoleon would triumph over the English king, for which he was tried as a traitor. Subsequently, as far as one can tell, he seems to have lost interest in politics.

The other concerned his role as a seer whose visions linked him to a tradition of ancient European beliefs that predated Christianity. To label his beliefs a form of neo-Platonism is perhaps to make them unnecessarily difficult; simply put, Blake held that all souls existed originally with god in heaven but descended to earth to don human flesh and live as fallen creatures. From there, however, they were destined again to cast off their human forms and ascend to heaven. Blake's notions of "innocence," the purity of the child who is closer than the adult to his soul in heaven, and "experience," which is the hard toil assigned to that innocent spirit, are the subject of his widely read collections *Songs of Innocence* and *Songs of Experience*.

After completing these unique first works, Blake brought out his "prophecies" in quick succession, illustrated with his highly idiosyncratic pictures and published in small hand-printed editions. Among the shorter of these is a strange but lovely poem called "The Book of Thel," which tells the story of an ethereal being who dwells in the valley of eternal life but wonders about her existence there and seeks to find answers to her doubts by questioning a lily, a cloud, and a worm. Finally, having consulted a lump of clay, she manages to pass through the gate leading to the world of men, but one look at this vale of tears sends her fleeing, with a piercing shriek, back to the valley of eternal life.

I found myself recalling this poem when my elder brother developed cancer, and especially Blake's description of the eternal realm, which has a kind of delicate beauty reflected in the accompanying prints. In plain, precise, and convincing words he is able to capture the desolation of the land of those doomed to die and the frailty of human flesh; he makes one think of all the hosts of people, with oneself among them, passing through this world only to fall victim to disease or to the ravages of age. My brother's cancer has spread to his liver and will soon kill him. As if unafraid of this other reality, the two of us used to laugh and sing together once; but now it is another sound we hear—the cries of pain that mark the true condition of our lives. . . .

Then, in a less despairing mood, I go on to think that maybe in a way we are like Thels who ventured down to this world but didn't go crying back to heaven; who, when they made that now-forgotten choice, perhaps told themselves to "just get on with it." In fact, the older I get—and I have reached the age when one begins to lose friends and family and start thinking of one's own death a few years hence—the more convinced I am that my soul, in that instant when it was first marked with the stain of mortal life, turned to face its fate with the same resolve.

An hour ago, as I was writing this, Hikari had a seizure, and I stopped to help my wife take care of him. Now he is recovering, stretched out on the couch next to my desk. Looking at his flushed, feverish face as he peers back at me, I can't avoid the painful thought that in his case he really was born with those words on his lips. But for the moment his pain seems to have passed and he is smiling to himself—the smile, surely, another sign of his willingness to accept things as they are.

# It's the Same in Every Family

THIS YEAR, as usual, we all made a card for my wife's birthday, and for mine I simply copied the following lines from the seventeenth-century English poet Robert Herrick, whose works I happened to be reading:

So Good-luck came, and on my roofe did light,
Like noyse-lesse Snow; or as the dew of night:
Not all at once, but gently, as the trees
Are, by the Sun-beams, tickel'd by degrees.

Our family tree, like most others, has seen its share of dark days and nights, but when all is said and done, sunlight usually comes filtering through onto each of its branches. And as these branches reach out to soak up the light, they can count on the trunk of the tree, my wife, to firmly hold them up. I wanted to say this to her directly, but found myself resorting to our family tradition of card-making, and borrowing Herrick's lines.

The message on Hikari's card, though, came as something of a surprise:

> Happy Birthday. It looks like the number of people turning 56 this year is gradually increasing. So take special care not to catch cold. Still, I can't write bigger than this. My writing is not too good.
>
> I like the evening every day. You bring dinner. It's the same in every family. By "evening" I mean five o'clock.
>
> My teeth are better and I go to the dentist every Wednesday. Still, I'm careful.
>
> I am not too scared.

Now Hikari has a rather serious temperament, and the occasions when he has clearly been angry with me can generally be traced to some sort of practical joke I've played on him. He has had this serious streak in him, moreover, since he was very young, and when he tries to be funny in something he is saying or writing, it is usually the product of an elaborate effort (though some of the humor is inevitably unconscious). At any rate, the logic in his card was faultless if a bit perverse: since it was the beginning of the year, the number of people turning fifty-six, the same age as his mother, would naturally continue to increase as the year went by. It was also true, of course, that the number of people turning fifty-seven was increasing, but part of Hikari's joke was in pretending to ignore that fact. In the final analysis, of course, he was right: the number of people turning fifty-six this year was gradually increasing. . . .

Another seemingly cryptic comment in his card concerned a subject much on Hikari's mind: dental hygiene. One of the ongoing and occasionally serious trials of his existence has been his teeth, a problem that has resulted in weekly Wednesday visits to the dentist. His teeth were uneven from the time he was a baby, and since he has never learned to brush them very well, they have constantly given him trouble. On one occasion he even had several teeth extracted under a general anesthetic, and I remember sitting in the waiting room feeling as tense as I had at that first operation after his birth. To make the whole situation worse, when he reached puberty, Hikari started having epileptic fits, and the medicine he takes to control them makes his gums red and lumpy, like strawberries. Since then, we've been reluctant to force him to brush, so a lot of his teeth are loose and his breath rather smelly.

I am pleased to report, however, that recently we have seen a remarkable improvement in that area, thanks to the careful instruction he and my wife received at the Dental Center in Umegaoka, an institution that has been a godsend to the mothers of handicapped children. As I watch the two of them every evening running through the battery of oddly shaped brushes, I can see that they have really taken it to heart. Once his gums started getting better, however, it became clear that more of the teeth would have to be pulled out and replacements made, a prospect that naturally caused Hikari a certain amount of anxiety. In fact, I have been up early today trying to finish a draft of this text before we go off to have a major piece of this work done; and it was no doubt to reassure his mother in this respect that Hikari wrote that he was "not too scared." That, then, explains the beginning and the end of his message; but what about the middle section?

My wife's mother, the widow of the film director Mansaku Itami, is in her late eighties and has lived with us for a number of years. Recently, as her mental faculties have deteriorated, she has developed the habit of emerging from her room next to the front door dozens of times a day to greet visitors who exist only in her head; on bad days these trips to the garden gate are repeated every four or five minutes from early in the morning until evening. If she finds the newspaper or any little scrap of advertising in the mailbox, she then comes to hand it over to me in the living room where I'm usually working or reading. Since she is an extremely proper and dignified person, she will stand, perfectly erect, clutching her offering and waiting for me to get up to receive it properly. Until a couple of years ago, even when she had nothing to deliver she would still come to ask after my health or something of the sort, but now she just rushes back and forth between the door and the gate. On rainy days the entranceway gets quite muddy, and I find myself worrying that she might fall and break a bone (as has actually happened before), but I know that nothing I could say would stop these frantic journeys that she keeps up throughout the day almost as if they were a form of exercise. Her comings and goings have been known to begin at dawn, but they grow noticeably more frequent in the late afternoon. One day, at the request of a counselor at a day care facility to which she has begun going, I recorded each of her appearances in the living room in the margin of the manuscript I was working on—I gave up somewhere after a hundred. Of all of us, however, Hikari seems to be the most sensitive to the signs of his grandmother's illness, and he watches her, looking obviously distressed, as he lies listening to music or working on his composing.

Eventually, though, at five o'clock, which is still too early for the rest of us to eat, my wife takes her mother's dinner to her room. As a rule, though there are exceptions, the end of her final meal of the day means the end of her trips to the gate—and the end of Hikari's worrying on her behalf, at least for another day. "I like the evening every day. You bring dinner. It's the same in every family. By 'evening' I mean five o'clock."

## 2

I think the thing that struck us most in Hikari's message, however, was his idea that "it's the same in every family." It has been a number of years since then, but there was a time when Hikari's grandmother, reticent though she was, occupied the center of our family circle. She was, moreover, particularly good to him, and their relationship was a kind of axis on which the rest of us turned. But as time passed she stopped joining in with us; and now, when she does make an appearance, it is just to deliver the newspaper or some advertising flier before disappearing again into her own room, where she watches with the door slightly ajar to see who is passing by. When Hikari is on his way up to his bedroom, she will pop out and talk to him, blocking his path. For Hikari, these interviews are difficult to understand, and he will generally stand in silence staring at the floor as she pesters him, for example, for news of her brother who died more than half a century ago, or tells him that he looks a good deal like her brother did, dressed in his officer's uniform. . . .

Lately, being too busy with other things, my wife and I rarely go into her room unless we're taking her a meal. Our daughter, too, after a tiring day in the university library, talks to her grandmother less frequently, and mostly on weekends. Is it, then, the isolation of the elderly that Hikari is referring to when he says "It's the same in every family"? This interpretation of his card, when it occurred to us, made us feel deeply ashamed; and since then, the time that my wife, at least, spends in her mother's room has increased considerably. The week the cherry trees in our neighborhood were in full bloom we decided to take her out for a look at them. As we were setting off, both my wife and her mother asked Hikari to look after the house. Stretched out in his usual place on the couch, listening to the radio, he didn't seem to take much notice, but . . .

I like to imagine a day when my mother-in-law will regain her mental faculties and her former energy, yet I know this is unlikely ever to happen. Hikari, too, has begun having powerful seizures recently and his health has been generally poor, meaning that we have to watch him all the more carefully on the way to and from the training center. To complicate matters, in April his brother will begin attending classes at the main campus of Tokyo University, so we can no longer count on him to help. And as for their aging father, I've begun to realize that when I take Hikari in the morning and pick him up in the afternoon, I spend much of the time in between recuperating on the couch rather than doing any work.

I remember, years ago, how natural it seemed to me that our family should be a hub of activity, and that it should go on like that forever; but now I can see that time has passed, that life and liveliness have dwindled, and occasionally I feel a wave of depression tinged with nostalgia sweep over me. In the old days, at the cottage in North Karuizawa, Hikari would drag his brother and sister off each morning for their "marathon"; and every evening, having finished his work, their father would jog down to the Kuma River at dusk to try his hand at trout fishing. Their mother would spend her days climbing the hills behind the cottage to pick the wild pinks and other flowers that later served as subjects for her sketches. Their grandmother, calling from another part of the country for her daily report on our doings, would greet each bit of news with obvious enthusiasm, as if she were celebrating some little triumph. . . .

But each phase of our lives passes, and we can't linger over memories. Frankly, we're just too busy to do so. Hikari has been attending the training center only sporadically of late, but when we turn up there we find them bustling around with preparations for their year-end festivities. And Hikari's teeth alone require almost full-time care. Each of us seems to be entering a new phase in his or her work or studies, while every afternoon, before the sun sets, my mother-in-law makes her endless circuits to the front gate. Still, though it may seem at times that something is always being lost or broken as our family rattles along day by day, it is just as certain that things also somehow get mended and rehabilitated. I have seen illustrations in medical texts of the cracked and withered brain of a senile person, and I suppose they should be taken as concrete evidence that my mother-in-law is unlikely to recover. But, taking a long view of things, she has made periodic improvements over the years; and don't all of us live in those moments, those periodic respites and recoveries with which we're blessed? And in the end aren't we all better off learning to take that long view?

# Sui Generis

               I REMEMBER the unexpected pleasure I felt some fifteen years ago when, in the course of a conversation, the writer Ryotaro Shiba mentioned Juzo Itami's name (this was well before Itami became known internationally for films like *The Funeral*, *Tampopo*, and *A Taxing Woman*) and spoke of his work with perception and enthusiasm. "He's a real *ijin*," Shiba had said to sum him up, without bothering to explain exactly what he meant; but having known Itami myself since we were in our teens, and being related to him by marriage, I felt that the comment was singularly accurate. All the same, I found myself going to my dictionary to check the meaning of this rather unusual word:

> **ijin**   1: Someone who is different from the norm; a superior person; "Each age gives birth to at least one extraordinary person" (Kyokutei Bakin, *Chinsetsu yumiharizuki*). 2: A different person; another person; a changed man. 3: A person who practices mysterious arts; a wizard. 4: A foreigner. (*Kojien*, 4th edition)

I happened to recall this conversation with Shiba when I was at the University of Chicago quite recently, where I'd been asked to give the centennial lecture at the Center for East Asian Studies. The lecture had been followed by a day-long discussion among various scholars, and during the lunch break I had taken advantage of the special library card they'd given me for the duration of my stay to go hunting for certain references. It was while I was there among the library stacks that members of the university film study group came to tell me that, back in Tokyo, Itami had been attacked by three thugs, apparently yakuza, and that his face and body had been slashed. I immediately called home and got the details from my wife, who seemed to have recovered from the shock by then, despite the fact that Itami was her brother. Later, she showed me the entries for those days in the diary she's been keeping for years: her main thought was that she was glad I was in the U.S. so she could spend as much time as she wanted visiting her brother in the hospital.

As I followed the various accounts and reactions in the

media (which until I got back to Japan amounted to little more than a well-researched, rather straightforward article in the *Los Angeles Times*), one feature stood out: the emphasis of the reports was not on the violence done to him by rightist thugs but on what they called the "anti-establishment" nature of his films. This led me to wonder just how genuinely "anti-establishment" his work actually is; how genuinely "anti-establishment" anything could be that supported the tax office and the police. As far as I can see, Itami doesn't seem to have taken a consciously "anti-establishment" position in his work—perhaps because it occurred to him that films by directors who are generally considered "anti-establishment" are for the most part extremely dull. First and foremost, I think, he is trying to make movies that are interesting and entertaining. His way of developing his concept, his attention to detail, and his considerable technical skill combine to create a vivid, individual kind of production; and if there is a "subversive" message there, it is one concealed in the fabric of the work.

2

Several years ago, on the day my mother-in-law was due to be admitted to a hospital for what had been diagnosed as tuberculosis, Itami came to drive her there in the elegant car he owns (his beloved Bentley, the same car he was attacked in when he was removing some luggage from the rear seat. The truth is that I believe it would have hurt him more had they damaged the car instead of him. Which itself is exactly the sort of slightly skewed fact of life—a hallmark of Itami's films as well as his everyday existence—that one sees so perfectly illustrated in details like the Rolls Royce-riding Buddhist priest in *The Funeral*.)

That day, for the first time in quite a while, I was able to have a long talk with him in his mother's comfortable hospital room. As we sat down for our chat, however, it was I who was still recovering from a rather unnerving experience, while Itami seemed the picture of composure. My distress resulted from a session with a hospital counselor who had been assigned to talk to me as the head of a household where a case of tuberculosis had been allowed to become quite serious. This woman had hauled me over the coals for my negligence: it wasn't just a matter of having neglected my mother-in-law's illness, I was in fact committing a crime against my own children by letting them live under the same roof as her—and, by extension, a crime against society as a whole. To make matters worse, since Grannie had behaved with great affability and even graciousness toward the doctor who was now treating her, it had been impossible to convince them that she had an almost morbid dread of hospitals. Itami had been present at this session, but, instead of defending me, he had sat and watched with the utmost unconcern. It was clear that the counselor knew perfectly well who he was—she was even, probably, a fan—and she went after me with almost missionary zeal, giving me a tongue-lashing on Itami's behalf for having maltreated his dear mother. Itami, I should add, once said in an interview in *The New York Times* that he thinks the people who live with his mother, given her personality, are a bit masochistic—a comment that caused some consternation among my American friends. This was, however, a period in which he was obsessed with psychology, even going so far as to coauthor a book with Freudians and Lacanians, and he seems to have decided that it had required an extraordinary effort on his part to achieve a measure of independence from the overprotective mother who had dominated him as a child. So, when he speaks of masochism on the part of the people who choose to live with this person (who continues, in fact, to be rather difficult), his remarks need to be understood in that context. I don't believe he intends any character attack on my wife and me. . . .

In any event, it was after his mother had submitted to a battery of tests and was installed in her room that Itami began to talk about something that he called the "grammar" of film. American movies, he said, generally had a strong sense of this "grammar" while Japanese films had almost none at all; but it was a quality he wanted to emphasize in his own work. (By coincidence, my daughter and I had recently been watching a series of big-budget American films —the kind I generally give a miss—which were broadcast on cable TV. One of them was *Back to the Future* Parts One, Two, and Three, and the thing that impressed me about it was precisely the elaborate and skillfully conceived plot. In the first installment, the story line was already quite ingenious; but they seem to have been determined to outdo themselves in Part Two, getting all the best scriptwriters in Hollywood to come up with an even better plot. And Part Three was more interesting still.) He also mentioned that, although the quality of his new film about the yakuza, *Minbo*, was quickly acknowledged even by Japanese critics who seemed to loathe him, it was, of course, necessary to do some extensive promotion for an expensive film like that, and Itami himself had been talking about it in the various media for some time before the incident. On such occasions, he had apparently discussed certain "steps one can take to avoid becoming a target of the yakuza" and other things of that kind, and no doubt there was a good deal of useful information in what he had to say, based as it was on his usual detailed research. But the sort of "practical measures against the mob" that Itami was cataloging in his lectures and television appearances to promote the film were subjected to considerable oversimplification by the media, so that the carefully considered points he was proposing were reduced to a caricature of a filmmaker's anti-gangster primer. At that point, misunderstandings were inevitable. There are, moreover, a lot of didactic films of this sort being made (though admittedly not about gangsters), so it may have been easier to subscribe to the mistaken view of Itami's project than to try to fully understand it. Itami's films, however, are multifaceted works that don't permit such simplification; and it is the business of the critic, in my opinion, to objectively reflect the actual qualities of a film and resist the sort of reductionism that is common in the media and advertising.

I am personally rather skeptical about the theory that the gangsters attacked Itami out of anger after actually seeing the movie. It seems more likely that they were spurred on by the advance publicity, which tended to miss the point of the film. Any superior work of art is one that, on the one hand, provokes powerful emotions while at the same time allowing the viewer to deal with those emotions within the context of the work itself, not by projecting them into the real world. And this is precisely the strategy followed in the highly developed plots of Itami's movies.

3

After my stay in Chicago, I gave some talks at campuses in Oahu and Hawaii. Since news from Japan tends to reach Hawaii more quickly than the mainland, a number of people kept me up-to-date on Itami's medical condition, on remarks he had made at press conferences, and so on. The thing that made the most impression on me among these reports was his comment that "freedom" was the main subject of his films and that he intended to carry on with this theme in the future. To me, this had the ring of truth to it, without any sort of "simplification."

When we first met, during our sophomore year at high school, Itami was already in the midst of a battle with the administration over the compulsory uniform rule. He'd found it impossible to ignore the matter of having to wear certain clothes every day, and he fought the rule relentlessly. In the end, he had to go on wearing the uniform, but he managed to cope by changing the standard gold buttons for black ones. Just recently, I spotted a picture of him giving a press conference in Europe, dressed in a Chinese-style jacket with a stand-up collar, and I was reminded of the way he looked forty years ago in that infamous uniform.

If one were to draw up a list of the things that infringe on our freedom—oppression, bigotry, discrimination, and the rest—it would be clear that Itami has suffered from most of them. I remember especially the time midway through our high school years when he quit school. Eventually, he decided he wanted to return, but his readmission was refused by the music teacher who was in charge of our class. Since it seemed clear that Itami wouldn't be able to speak for himself, I went along as his spokesman. I can still hear his voice, as I pleaded his case to the unyielding teacher, saying "It's OK, Kensanro" —my nickname at the time—"let's go." I realize now that if that teacher all those years ago had relented and let him back in, Itami would have prepared for his college entrance exams with the rest of us, and would ultimately have encountered the sort of minds that could have satisfied his natural thirst for knowledge. In the event, he went to work as an illustrator, and there is little doubt that this experience "fertilized" his later work as a director; but there might have been a smoother, happier way for him to have realized his potential.

4

Itami was released from the hospital soon after the attack and lost no time in collecting material for his next film, without any apparent aftereffects from his ordeal. He and his wife, the actress Nobuko Miyamoto, came by to bring us some of the flowers he was given by friends and acquaintances, and in the course of their visit the conversation came around to the subject of some rather nasty things that were currently being said . . . this time about me; not, however, by yakuza but by a certain member of the Academy of the Arts. Nobuko decided that the women would have to start protecting their men, and, with a laugh, my levelheaded wife agreed.

Here, we recognized on our side, was another "healing family" whose upbeat mood we too could share.

Yukari

*Hikari as a baby, with toys*

*Hikari with his younger brother and sister (North Karuizawa)*

*Dr. Moriyasu and Hikari*

*Rehearsal with Hiroshi Koizumi*

'92 Yukari

*Objects on K. Oe's desk*

*The hotel in Salzburg*

*Vienna*

*Hikari*

# Well-Chosen Words

I HAVE ALWAYS been fascinated to hear people talking about themselves. But recently it occurred to me to wonder just what sort of people were really interesting to listen to, and I came up with the following categories: people who know a great deal about many different things; people who have been to a "new world"; and, of course, people who have experienced something strange or frightening. As much as I enjoy hearing people talk about their experiences, however, it is extremely difficult to listen attentively to someone who is simply laying out his or her knowledge in a particular field of specialization, the sort of knowledge, moreover, that most of us acquire in one degree or another in the normal course of events. At any rate, while I could probably produce a long list of actual examples, the simple fact is that I prefer to listen to people who use "well-chosen words." By this I don't mean highly elaborate technical language, but rather the speech of someone who uses a few carefully selected terms in which to frame whatever he or she has to say. One has the feeling, hearing it, of encountering a fresh sort of intelligence, and, much later, the words themselves serve to remind one of the conversation as a whole.

But in what way, exactly, do these "well-chosen words" make someone's conversation more interesting? In some cases, they seem to be chosen on the basis of extensive study or research; in others, to derive from a lifetime's experience; but more common than either of these singly are the cases where both expertise and experience combine.

All of this brings me to an example of someone outstanding in this regard: our friend Akiko Ebi, the gifted pianist who played on the first recording of Hikari's compositions, *The Music of Hikari Oe* (CO-78952). It is some time now since I first began reading her articles in magazines and program notes and realized how carefully she chose her words, her writing giving one the same sense of well-being that a conversation with this calm and lovely woman does.

Among her favorite words, apparently, are the verbs "perceive" and "feel." We may *know* something about flowers or trees, she says; we may *know* about human beings or the universe itself through an act of the intellect. But only when we truly come to understand these things through experience or imagination do we realize that we had never properly *perceived* them. That, I think, is what I believe she means by insisting on the word "perceive"—a term that comes close to *connaître* in French, a language she happens to speak quite well.

Another of her special idioms is the phrase "to be moved by." When, for instance, a musician is really moved by the music of Debussy or Chopin, then, for the first time, he or she can make that music a form of self-expression. Though the verb is passive in mood, Akiko Ebi seems to imbue it with an active sense, giving it greater intensity.

At an early age, she went to study music in France, and after winning some major prizes in important competitions, she remained in Europe for a number of years to give concerts. Presumably the ability to speak French would have been a valuable skill for coping with that demanding situation; and this she had, not only carrying on her everyday life in French but also communicating with conductors, fellow musicians, audiences, and critics in that language. (It is worth pointing out that this is an extremely rare achievement among Japanese intellectuals.) But for those few who, like Ms. Ebi, have managed to make a career abroad, it is generally the case that they develop, conversely, a special feeling for their mother tongue, which becomes a touchstone for them, a means of reflection when living in a foreign country. And since Japanese is itself so very vague, I imagine they feel a need to redefine or revise certain words or fine-tune their usage.

For me, however the most extraordinary thing about Akiko Ebi is that as much as I enjoy her choice of language, I find even greater pleasure in listening to her piano give voice to the music she has so distinctively "perceived" and been "moved by" herself. This is especially true when she has played Hikari's music for us at home. The extent to which she has perceived and been moved by the things that are in his heart becomes apparent then; and, equally, the intensity with which Hikari listens to her playing suggests that he too is then perceiving the things that matter most in this world.

2

Among Hikari's most memorable experiences must surely be our trips to the studios of Nippon Columbia for recording sessions with Ms. Ebi and Hiroshi Koizumi—sessions he attended as the composer. On the first day, we took the subway to Akasaka and followed a map to the studio; but the walk through an unfamiliar neighborhood, combined with the excitement of anticipation, must have worn him out, and while we were waiting for the elevator he had a seizure. Thus, as the sound of a piano being tuned drifted in from the studio next door, my wife and I found ourselves holding damp towels to his forehead and lining up chairs for him to lie down on. Once the recording started, however, he recovered enough to play his allotted role, though in a manner that was a bit more subdued than it might have been.

Before we came to this session, Hikari and his music

teacher had already subjected the scores to repeated and careful scrutiny, and all the pieces, moreover, were relatively simple in terms of technique. Still, while rehearsing them on her own, Ms. Ebi had come up with a number of questions about harmonics and had several proposals for the treatment of the rests; she also wanted to check with Hikari on details such as tempo and emphasis in staccato sections. Listening to her questions as they came through the speakers from the studio, Hikari would think for a brief moment and then provide a precise answer to each. In some cases, she would play a passage in two or three different styles and ask Hikari which he preferred; he invariably made his choice without hesitation and never seemed to waver or have second thoughts about his decisions. This kind of immediate, crystal-clear communication between the pianist and Hikari was made possible by a shared language of "well-chosen words" based directly on music itself; and thanks in large part to this sort of refreshingly smooth and unambiguous exchange, everyone—the technicians included—seemed to enjoy the session, lengthy though it was.

A newspaper reporter had also come to cover the recording. He seemed to be well disposed, with a sincere interest in Hikari's music, but when he began, slowly and patiently, to question him about the process of composing and what he wanted to express in his music, Hikari simply cocked his head on one side and said nothing. Even when I stepped in to try to make sure Hikari was understanding what was being asked, he failed to come up with anything that the reporter found worth writing down. For me, this exchange, or lack of one, illustrated the fact that lines of communication can prove far more difficult to establish in everyday conversation than in a technical discussion. Though it may sound paradoxical, the ambiguities and opacity that characterize ordinary speech make failures in communication more common than might be expected. Moreover, in order to proceed smoothly, everyday language requires a background of shared experience between the speaker and the listener. In contrast, technical terminology is designed to be used by any competent speaker as a neutral tool to accurately convey information. Of course, it takes an effort to learn it, but once it has been mastered it is an extremely efficient means of communication. Hikari and Ms. Ebi had this in common, while the reporter and Hikari were adrift on the murky sea of conventional speech. . . .

When the recording was over, we had to confirm the titles for each of the numerous short pieces in order to finalize the liner notes for the CD. Ever since he started composing, Hikari has come up with an appropriate title for each of his pieces soon after completing it, writing it neatly at the top of the score before filing it carefully away. To date, his works include: "Graduation," "Birthday Waltz," "Ave Maria," "Bluebird March," "Star," "Waltz in A Minor," "Rondo," "Summer in Kitakaru," and "Mister Prelude." This last, it seems, is his tribute to Bach, the author of so many famous preludes. When Dr. Moriyasu died, he composed two pieces for his widow: "Requiem for M" and "Lullaby for Keiko." In addition, there are works called "Dance," "Siciliano," "Ländler," and "Grief." And, last but not least, he wrote a piece when my wife and I went to Europe once and left Hikari at home: "May the Plane Not Fall."

As is apparent from this list, he had named a number of things after generic forms of European dance music, and these tended to overlap one another. So we asked him to think up some new titles, which resulted in "Magic Flute" and "A Favorite Waltz," the first for a piece that shares a certain mood with Mozart's opera and the latter for a tune that my wife is particularly fond of and often hums to cheer herself up. Hikari had very little to say while these discussions were going on, but he seemed to be thinking carefully about the mood in each piece of music and listening attentively to what was being said about them. Then, when asked, he was able to come up with a "well-chosen" title for each one; and in the end we all came to feel that the ones he'd devised had a kind of indisputable appropriateness to them, though often for unexpected reasons, and the more we listened to the music itself, the more this feeling took hold.

3

Some time ago, the whole family made a trip back to the village in the woods of Shikoku where I was born. While we were there, Hikari spent a lot of the time with his grandmother, to whom he grew very attached. On the flight home, however, I noticed that my daughter seemed upset about something, and it eventually came out that Hikari was to blame. Apparently his rather boisterous farewell to his grandmother had been:

"Cheer up and have a good death!"

"Right you are," she'd answered, "I will! But it's sad to have to say good-bye. . . ."

Soon after we got back, having talked things over with his sister, Hikari put in a call to set things straight. I remember how we all gathered around the phone, trying to hear how his grandmother was reacting on the other end of the line. "I'm very sorry," Hikari told her. "I said the wrong thing before. Cheer up and have a good life!" From what we could tell, my mother laughed and accepted his apology. The point of this story, though, is that sometime after our visit she fell seriously ill; fortunately, she recovered, but she told my sister, who nursed her through it, that while she was sick the thing that had most encouraged her to go on fighting it, oddly enough, was Hikari's farewell to her—in the original version. She remembered just how he had shouted "Cheer up and have a good death!" to her. And that, she said, was probably what had made her pull through.

Hikari is usually pretty quiet when he is at home. During our visit to Shikoku, too, I can imagine that he mostly listened while my mother talked; and it seems likely that she made some remark to him about how she'd grown old, how she'd lived a full life but now had nothing left to do but die, and how she hoped she could do it with some dignity. . . . My sister, at least, claims to have heard her saying such things more than once. If Hikari heard them too, then they must have stirred up some very troubling thoughts, which he turned over and over in his mind until, like someone skimming off bubbles floating up out of the gloom, he found these "well-chosen words"; and he stored away in his head until, as he was saying good-bye to her, they popped out of his mouth. Then, later, this memorable message from her handicapped grandson had helped her to survive her illness.

I, for one, plan to remember Hikari's parting words for that inevitable day when my own time comes as well.

# Disabled Persons Decade

IN JAPAN LATELY it has become something of a convention for novelists to give "talks," and as a result I have got rather used to phone calls from the people who arrange these things. Often enough, they fancy themselves "producers," and their manner on the phone reflects this image: "Are you free on such and such a day?" they'll ask, without any preamble. "We're putting together a talk show. . . ." I remember one young woman in particular who phoned with one such request, and, as was always the case, once I'd picked up the receiver I found it difficult to say no. I told her that from my time in America I remembered watching "talk shows" on late-night TV, and I associated them with protracted, largely vacuous verbal sparring that was often spiced with racial hatred—not exactly my cup of tea, I assured her as best I could. "Oh, no," she insisted, "that's not what we have in mind at all. We're trying to create a new kind of forum for cultural exchange. We're working with a woman who used to be the editor of a weekly magazine, lining up just the right sort of people for her to talk to. . . ." Her answer was glibly pervasive, and it was all I could do—and time-consuming, too—to finally refuse.

Novelists, by the nature of their work, are people for whom an outside engagement or a trip is the exception rather than the rule. Stay-at-home days with, apparently at least, "nothing" to do are bread and butter for a writer, our most indispensable sort of days. Not long ago I had a call from the South African Nobel laureate, Nadine Gordimer, and went to meet her at her hotel. "What," she wondered aloud, "is more important for us than writing novels?" Yet, we commiserated, there were always so many things getting in the way.

This explains why I have reached the point where I no longer accept requests for lectures or speeches unless they come from close friends or my publishers; or, when someone does call, why I make it a habit to ask him to send his request in writing with an explanation of the purpose of the event, before I decide. The lecture I gave in Sakai City at the end of last year is a happy example of this procedure. I believe the call came at the beginning of the summer, and in response to my request a letter followed from a Mr. M of the Handicapped Welfare Department there. The letter had a special resonance for people in our situation:

> At the end of this special U.N. decade of the disabled, during which we have heard calls for equality and social integration for all handicapped people, those who are most closely connected with these issues—the handicapped themselves—look to the future with a mixture of hope and apprehension. Will the official, and popular, interest and concern they've received in the past ten years continue? Or, as has always been the case in the past, will they again be pushed out of sight, relegated to some virtually invisible corner of the collective consciousness?
>
> During the last ten years, the growing awareness of their existence has highlighted our tendency to lose sight of what it means to have real sympathy for our fellow human beings; the disabled have shown us, all too clearly, the narrowness of our outlook. It has been said that "the society that excludes the disabled is by definition a feeble, fragile one." I feel we should re-examine what this means, see in what way exactly such a society is weak.

His letter went on to discuss a conference he was inviting me to participate in.

> It seems to me that this notion of the "acceptance of the handicapped as a problem for the community," which

we're asking you to speak about, inevitably goes beyond being merely a "problem" for the individual or the family and addresses the question of how society as a whole is going to learn to accept and live together with its handicapped members. The fact is that, in the very act of learning to do this, all of us—not just the handicapped—become measurably freer; and this, to my mind, suggests an opportunity for the creation of the "new kind of humanity" that you yourself have often spoken of.

Not surprisingly, I agreed to take part and sent off an outline of what I intended to say.

## 2

I had already given the questions M raised some thought: first, as to why a society that shuts out this part of itself can be considered a "feeble, fragile one." I can only speak on the basis of my experience of the one model I've seen of a community that does *not* shut out the handicapped, namely, that of the University of California at Berkeley where I once spent some time. The campus is built on the side of a mountain, and the difference in elevation from one end to the other is so extreme that one could almost imagine they had to import vegetation from various altitudes to insure that it would grow in the various microclimates. But while this unique topography makes for spectacular views, one can't help thinking it would prove a major obstacle for those with physical disabilities. Nevertheless, at Berkeley it isn't at all uncommon to see people crisscrossing the campus in motorized wheelchairs at remarkable speeds.

Where, I wondered to myself, would these handicapped students (and among them were some with mental disabilities as well) have gone if Berkeley had shut them out? Some of them, no doubt, would have gone home to live in seclusion; others would have been institutionalized. Now I am the first to recognize that institutions are sometimes necessary and, if properly run, can even serve as staging grounds for the integration of the disabled into society at large. Furthermore, if the handicapped are able to lead active, meaningful lives in such institutions, that in itself is evidence of the vitality of the society that sets them up. No doubt there have always been institutions of this sort; and no doubt we should regard such places themselves as models of an "open society." But it is equally true that there have been and in all probability still are places that have as their express purpose—or their effective result—the isolation of the handicapped, functioning thus as the necessary complements to a closed society.

Flannery O'Connor once wrote something to the effect that sentimental attitudes toward handicapped children, which encourage the habit of hiding their pain from human eyes, are of a piece with the kind of thin' ng that sent smoke billowing from the chimneys of Auschwitz. I would venture to guess, in fact, that many parents of handicapped children would hesitate to dismiss this comparison as a grotesque exaggeration. These are people who are constantly aware that their own aging or sudden death can only mean that their children will be sent to an institution; and for them the thought that there are well-run, open institutions is of little comfort.

On a more personal level, I can imagine a very concrete example of what happens to a society that shuts out its disabled by asking myself how we ourselves—the Oes—would have turned out if we hadn't made Hikari an indispensable part of our family. I imagine a cheerless house where cold drafts blow through the gaps left by his absence; and, after his exclusion, a family whose bonds grow weaker and weaker. In our case, I know it was *only* by virtue of having included Hikari in the family that we actually managed to weather our various crises, such as my mother-in-law's gradual mental decline.

Interestingly enough, the very fact that one of our number is handicapped has meant that the rest of us have learned to improvise rather creatively to compensate. Over the years, for example, Hikari's sister has had to devise innumerable ways to jolly him out of his foul moods. Despite this long apprenticeship, however, she volunteered for work with the disabled at college, and this outside experience helped her take a more knowledgeable and systematic approach to looking after him, while also teaching her to distance herself from him when necessary in order to say the kind of difficult things that need saying. In short, I think she came to see him not only as a disabled member of our family but as a disabled member of society. There is, even now, in the way she relates to Hikari, a shadow of their childhood, of the little girl who thought up all sorts of schemes for coaxing him out for a walk; yet without in any way denying that past, she has developed into a mature and capable young woman, perhaps most of all where her brother is concerned.


### 3

So it was while I was preparing my response to M's letter for the conference that I saw how closely integrated the problem of private and public acceptance of a disability is. It all became rather easier to grasp, I felt, when one thought of society as a family writ large; the trick, as it were, was to model a society's actions—all its best efforts—on those of the family that has actively welcomed a handicapped child into its midst. Eventually, that sort of family, through its own process of acceptance, can come to play a special role in the community immediately surrounding it; and in time this can send a message to a much wider group.

# Yujo

AS A GENERAL RULE, I am not in favor of novelists coining new words. The situation for poets is somewhat different, since they are, in a sense, pioneers at the frontiers of language. It is their duty, one feels, to bring back the words they discover there to introduce them to the world at large—at which point, and not before, they become available to the novelist. However, there have been occasions when I've found myself filing away a special word, together with the new meaning a novelist has given it, for later, albeit very careful, use in my own work. One example of this is the term *yujo*, which consists of two Chinese characters that aren't traditionally paired but, taken together, mean something like the "warmth" (*jo*) of a "gentle sort of humanity" (*yu*); it doesn't involve the homonyms "friendship" or "sentience" (*yujo*), and yet there is a sense of its being a combination of the two. In this particular case, I suspect there were a number of scouts who could claim to have first sighted this word somewhere on the fringes of language and brought it back for use as standard Japanese, but in my internal lexicon it is recorded as the discovery of the novelist Yoshie Hotta.

Under the title "If Goya Were to Paint a Gentle Giant," I tried to capture the character of this man in a piece I wrote for a promotional brochure when a new edition of his collected works came out:

> The year I spent living in an old dormitory at Berkeley was passed in the shadow of a great oak tree; and often, when I looked at it, I found myself thinking of Hotta: a massive, upright trunk, branches spreading wide in all directions, and the vast root system stretching off in the darkness underground. But even more than these, it was the dense foliage that conjured up in my mind the image of Hotta's life as a writer.
>
> Nadine Gordimer has suggested that a writer does not choose his own themes, but rather, as a sort of consciousness of his age, is himself chosen, and his commitment is determined by the way in which he handles these themes. Her comment, I feel, precisely describes

the career of Yoshie Hotta. Gordimer goes on to say that each one of an individual writer's works contributes to the larger project of telling the story of what it means to be human; and that, again, is precisely what Hotta did. He traveled the world of Japan's middle ages, of medieval Europe, the Renaissance, and Goya's age—the history and things transcending history—quite at his ease, recounting the human story. Moreover, his own life, starting in China and passing through the plains of postwar Japan, was a moving tale worthy of any novel, while his prose is the most subtle sort of music, sung by a strange though supremely human giant, a giant who dwells among us.

Let me repeat myself, then: Hotta himself embodies this term, *yujo*, which he invented, and yet never once, in the travels we made together through India, Uzbekistan, and Thailand, did I see anything sweet or cloying in his brand of "gentleness." This aspect of his personality coexisted with a rigor that was at the very core of his nature; nor do I mean by that the old saw that he was strict with himself but gentle with others. Hotta was stern with everyone, himself included, as a function of the fundamental meaning of *yujo*; but, by the same token, no matter how strict he was, he could never be cruel.

## 2

More than twenty years ago, I was staying with Hotta in

Benares in an old colonial hotel. I remember I was having afternoon tea—the likes of which I have never seen before or since—which had been brought to my room, tea cozy and all, with tremendous dignity by an enormous waiter. Hotta, who had grown up in the household of a foreign missionary (whose wife, I'm told, was rather fond of her drink) and was thus quite comfortable with English, was off in his own room listening to the BBC World Service, as he had been at that hour throughout our trip. I was stretched out on the bed reading a collection of Rabindranath Tagore's poetry and sipping tea when a call came from Hotta: "It seems Mishima has forced his way into army headquarters in Tokyo and committed ritual suicide," he said. "Well then, see you at dinner." As I frantically spun the radio dial looking for news, I marveled at how restrained, even cool, his announcement had been; and yet, when I went down to dinner in the restaurant with its view of the sun setting behind the crown of a huge banyan tree, there was Hotta in a dark blue suit and black tie, his version of mourning. It is the basic attitude indicated by this behavior that I would call *yujo*.

At one point Hotta spent a considerable amount of time in Spain. On his return, he came and presented me with a souvenir of Barcelona: a porcelain ornament. Now, as everyone knows, in this age when foreign travel has become a commonplace event (though one, I like to think, that still holds the possibility of being a life-transforming experience), the most bothersome thing of all to bring home is a heavy, breakable, and rather bulky piece of pottery—exactly what Hotta had decided to bring. It was a hedgehog: a wheat-brown body in which a white muzzle with black eyes and a black tail were buried. The body was long and narrow and heavier than it looked, and the sides were mottled and pocked. The note from Hotta that accompanied it suggested that since I was interested in calligraphy I might use it as a paperweight.

I have found a place for this creature on the shelf in front of my desk, and, since its arrival, not a day goes by when I don't commune with it. In fact, I wrote the passage for the brochure quoted above while examining this calm and comic bit of brown and white clay, which is often the occasion for my recalling the useful notion of *yujo*. I almost feel nowadays that there is some sort of family connection between this gift and its giver. I imagine Hotta on a street in Spain where such pottery is produced, stopping suddenly and reaching out his hand; and, for me at least, there is nothing very odd in the idea that there should be an affinity between this little hedgehog and that giant writer.

3

I have been writing here about Hotta, his word, and the hedgehog in part because I wanted to put down a few reflections on the other objects that share space with it on the shelf in my study. In this four-foot-long universe, each thing is linked to a particular "gentle" memory from my own travels in various countries, or to memories of the friends who brought them back for me. Among the pieces in this collection, the one that seems most fragile—likely, in fact, to break right before your eyes—is a frog, all of about two inches long, that consists of a baked clay head to which a paper sack has been attached as a kind of sound box—though the toy has long since lost its voice. It is something I bought at a stall in front of the ruins of Borobudur in Indonesia.

At some point after I turned forty, I made a "study trip" of sorts to the island of Bali with some friends. We went at the invitation of Japan Airlines, which sent its own representative along with us. The initial idea for the trip was, in fact, his: he thought it would be interesting to have people from different fields of inquiry—a professor of French literature and a film director who had been his classmates at the University of Tokyo, as well as a few scholars, artists, and others—gather somewhere to discuss a particular region "on site," as it were.

In any event, during what promised to be a stimulating trip I ran into a rather comic problem. It happened that my departure for Bali very nearly coincided with the date I was due to give my editor the manuscript of *A Contemporary Game*, and in the rush I went off to Narita airport having added nothing more to the suitcase my wife had packed for me than a few books to read, a procedure that wasn't unusual in hurried moments. On settling into the hotel in Jakarta and deciding to go down to change some money to buy a book on Bali in the lobby bookstore, I discovered that my wife (who had been pretty busy herself) had forgotten to put the cash for my traveling expenses in my bag. Fortunately, I also discovered an envelope, tucked into the book I was reading, containing the honorarium for a television appearance I'd made with an American writer the day before. Now this was an extremely lucky find, for while our travel expenses were being covered by JAL, we were each expected to pay for our own meals and accommodation; yet as I looked in the envelope, I remembered with chagrin how the American, on checking his, had commented that he had heard the Japanese were "modest," as he put it, about these things, and that the contents confirmed the rumor. Still, a quick calculation told me that it would be just enough for my basic expenses, and I found myself feeling very grateful even for such a "modest" sum.

Looking back on it, I suppose my traveling companions must have decided I was rather frugal. I bought one book at the first hotel but did virtually no shopping after that. In the afternoons, when we were generally free to do as we liked, I went swimming in the hotel pool. In practice, though, my spartan ways were not very different from the rest of our group's, since we were a serious bunch of people and tended to spend our evenings in earnest discussion rather than out in pursuit of the exotic local female population—a fact that wasn't lost on the locals: we heard later that one of the guides was convinced we were a gay tour group. . . .

My financial troubles aside, the most lasting memory I have of Bali is connected with a young woman I encountered at a Pura Dalem ("Temple of Death"), one of the cluster of three temples in each village. The guardian deity of the Pura Dalem is a sorceress named Rangda who is said to take possession of her victims and cause them great harm but who also uses her magic to cure illness. We arrived at the temple at sunset, just as the rain was letting up, and while we were having a look around the grounds I noticed the lovely profile of a young woman who was praying quietly while her younger siblings waited nearby. It was only after we had finished the tour and were leaving that I realized I'd left my notebook behind and had to return to the precincts of the temple to retrieve it. As I did so, the young woman and her charges passed me on their way out, and I saw what she had skillfully concealed until then: the other side of her beautiful face was so badly deformed that it stopped me in my tracks.

I wondered how many evenings, for how many years, she had come, her brothers and sisters in tow, to ask Rangda to heal her. I was somehow deeply moved, and I couldn't help thinking of Hikari who, had he been born in a farming family in Bali, might also have passed his evenings praying to Rangda to heal his brain. And something told me that these peaceful prayers, regardless of their efficacy, would have been among his greatest pleasures.

But I am telling this story because I wanted to write about the objects on my desk—and the one souvenir I bought on this pauper's journey: a clay frog, painted mud brown with eyes and mouth outlined in silver. When you pulled on the head, attached to the body by a paper accordion, it let out a croak that was exactly like the ones we'd heard coming from paddies and rivers throughout Indonesia. I found a whole row of these treasures at a stall that occupied the very best position in the square at the bottom of the steps leading down from the Buddhist temple of Borobudur. Curious as to why these odd creatures should have pride of place there,

I had stopped in front of the stand just as the proprietor, a middle-aged man in a faded, long-sleeved shirt of Javan calico, made one of his creations give a little croak, no doubt to attract our attention. It was then I noticed that the hand protruding from his sleeve had a sixth finger attached to it like a spur; and it occurred to me that it was probably thanks to this one small deformity that this unassuming man had been able to secure such favorable conditions for his business at one of Indonesia's most popular tourist sites.

Again, my thoughts turned to Hikari: had he been born in Java, mightn't he too have been given a similar spot in which to make his living in accordance with his own handicap? As I stood in the shade of a tamarind tree, I remembered how the few handicapped people in our village in the forest when I was a boy had each, in a sense, been given just such a spot and had joined fully in our communal life.

It remains, then, to explain the link in my thoughts between this frog and the notion of *yujo* with which I started, and it comes down to this: what better example of "gentle humanity" could you find than a rough, hardheaded group of vendors in a sun-baked square in Java giving the best place to their six-fingered colleague?...

4

Another object, a treasure that has been there for quite some time, is a model of a castle made for me by Kazuo Watanabe, the specialist in French literature. The date on the tag attached to it reveals that he was sixty-nine when he made it. That year the final volume of his collected works had been published, and the model was his way of acknowledging my part in the editing of this project. The European-style castle, which was chiseled out of a piece of slate, is painted white with orange-brown conical roofs on the turrets. On the base is a lovely painted crest, with the legend "Manoir du Grand-Duc Oë en Utopie"; below it is an inscription.

The first of the banners merely combines the letters $O$ and $E$. The blue and white fields of the second banner boast a venerable lineage: these are the heraldic colors of Lord Gargantua, whom François Rabelais called into being. Blue for the sky, the sublime; white for joy and laughter. (*Gargantua*, Chapter 10)

The crest of the Grand-Duc Oë is derived from that of François 1$^{er}$. The figure seated calmly in the red flame is the legendary Salamander, which eats fire but is never itself consumed; this beast was beloved of King François who caused its image to be emblazoned throughout his palace and on his various personal effects. In the language of heraldry, custom has it that the flame that enfolds this Salamander is known as "Patience"—a designation of great significance.

"Nutrisco et Exstinguo," too, is the motto of François 1$^{er}$. Although it is clearly linked in meaning to the Salamander's role, it also speaks of the dark ambitions of kings and princes of old. Translated literally it means "I nurture and destroy"; in the case of Grand-

Duc Oë, however, by virtue of his great discretion and integrity, this can be interpreted in the sense of nurturing what is good and destroying what is bad.

Reading this for the first time in some years produced a surge of different feelings, among them surprise at the extraordinary care he'd taken over it. The campus of Rikkyo University where he had set up a department of French literature happened to be quite near the hospital where Hikari was taken when he was born, and on my way home from one of my daily visits to the pediatric intensive care unit— visits which were obviously quite different from ordinary hospital sick calls—I'd decided to drop in on him. The professor was in a good mood, or was at least pretending to be, when I arrived. At the University of Tokyo where he had taught for most of his career, he hadn't had an office of his own, "but here at Rikkyo, as you can see . . ." He gestured around, feigning satisfaction. Then he gave the back of a Windsor rocking chair a push to set it in motion for my benefit, but in the cramped space it hit the corner of the desk. At that point, like a small child wailing to a parent, I launched into the story of the birth of this boy with a growth at the back of his skull, without a thought for the distress I was likely to cause my listener. The sight of the professor's noble profile flushing red almost as soon as I started speaking is something I will never forget.

In *A Personal Matter*, the novel I wrote based on Hikari's birth, the protagonist's first reaction is to try to flee from his deformed child. After many a twist and turn, however, he finally comes to the decision to make it part of his life, though it will almost certainly be retarded, and to take the word "patience" as his motto, the basis for his existence. It may seem odd, but I have only just now made the connection between that scene in the book and the fact that Watanabe's inscription identified the flame in the crest as "Patience." Now, too, I am reminded that he went to the trouble of boring a hole at the back of the castle and sticking a little label next to it that read: "Escape hatch." I also remember that a conversation between him and a writer who had been ahead of me in the French department was published somewhere, in which he said that he'd made the hole "because people like that" (he meant me) "need an escape hatch from time to time." With hindsight, I feel he was reminding me that, although one has a responsibility to stick things out to the limit of one's endurance, one also has to have the courage to retreat and lick one's wounds, so as to return to the fray refreshed.

# To Salzburg and Vienna

BY WAY OF an introduction to our trip to Austria, I would like to quote something I wrote in the program for the Berlin Opera's performances in Japan in the autumn of 1993.

> Though I have been familiar with Wagner's music since I was quite young, I have always felt there was a wall, a blockage of some kind that prevented me from being genuinely absorbed in it. This may be due, in part, to the fact that Yukio Mishima was devoted to his music. But the recent experience of hearing this

composer's work in the opera houses of Europe has compelled me, almost without realizing, to make a re-adjustment.

After a great deal of anticipation, a CD of my son's music was released in the fall of last year. In response to this event, several good friends of ours invited us—Hikari, my wife, and myself—to come to Europe just to listen to music. While we were extremely grateful for the invitation, our first inclination was to refuse. We had no precedent for this kind of journey in our experience as a family, no custom that made it seem possible. But one day, when Hikari wasn't able to go to his training center and we were listening to his CD, he said something—one of the jokes he tells from time to time—that made us reconsider: "I have been living for more than thirty years," he intoned in his best deadpan voice, "but my Total Playing Time is just forty-seven minutes, fifty-three seconds." It was at that moment that we decided we should take him on what would most likely be a once-in-a-lifetime journey. . . .

When discussing the process in *Tristan and Isolde* whereby the violent upsurge of love becomes entwined with the notion of an ecstatic death, a scholarly acquaintance of mine used the term "love-death" for this conjunction. In Europe, as we were listening to the soprano and tenor, I found myself thinking about the things these fictional lovers would learn when they reached my age, an age when one thinks almost daily about death but when love tends to be just a fond but distant memory. Yet, with something of a thrill, I had to admit that, as one comes to the end of one's life, there can in fact be a resurgence of their passionate approach to both love and death, bound inextricably together in an almost mystical way. And it was Wagner, needless to say, who made me acknowledge this unexpected truth.

While the trip as a whole was imbued with the spirit of Mozart and Beethoven, in Vienna we were presented with tickets for the third night of *The Ring of the Nibelung* at the State Opera House. To be frank, my wife and I wondered how well our son would cope with a five-hour performance, but our fears were unfounded. . . . There is a scene near the end of the opera where Hagen offers Siegfried a goblet of wine and slyly questions him: "I have heard that you understand the language of birds. . . ," he says. To which Siegfried, who still retains a certain innocence, replies: "For a long while now, I have paid no heed to their voices. . . ." As I have often written elsewhere, for the first four or five years of my son's life he never once uttered a coherent word, until one day he said "That's a water rail," which was something he had heard repeated on a record of a hundred different birdcalls we had given him. This first step on the narrow road to communication led almost immediately to music. Like Siegfried, he eventually seemed to forget the sound of birdsong. And yet, listening to Wagner, I felt it still spoke to him through the music. He listened, rapt, almost as if breathing it in. And even I, though never quite free of the weight of European culture that comes with it, could share some of his wonder at the incendiary spectacle of "love-death" at the heart of Wagner's music.

At the end of our journey, in the Quai d'Orsay Museum, I found myself walking straight up to Renoir's portrait of Wagner, a painting I hadn't known existed before, as if I had been counting on this meeting. And there, in the stern, bright, kind green eyes, I recognized a man I had only encountered for the first time on this trip.

2

The biggest adventure for our household in a decade, perhaps two, was made possible by the convergence of a number of chance yet necessary factors. (Now that I have passed fifty, experience has taught me to have great respect for this potent combination: chance and necessity.) One of these factors, unfortunate yet fortunate as well, was that my mother-in-law was recovering from a broken hip (the second time this had happened to her); the other was that our younger son, who is now studying agriculture, and our daughter, who has a job in the library of her alma mater, were both available to look after things while we were gone. Still, it wouldn't have been possible to leave my mother-in-law on her own during the day, past ninety and senile as she is; and so, though her accident was a setback, the fact that she was now hospitalized, with nursing care, created the necessary opening for our trip.

In addition to this, there was my work schedule to contend

with and some health problems my wife was having, but even as these resolved themselves and we actually began to make travel plans, we still had some concerns: would Hikari be able to stand the long flight, and how would he adjust to life in a hotel for nearly three weeks? Up until the time Hikari was about ten, my wife often used to take him to visit her parents' home in western Japan, where his grandmother generally made a fuss of him. In those days my wife was confident she could handle him on her own when they were out in public, on a plane or a train; and later, of course, travel became much easier when we got his conscious cooperation. But on the rare occasions when he did give her trouble, my wife was no longer capable of controlling him. Worse still, when he began having epileptic seizures, she wasn't even able to prop him up and keep him from falling in the street.

In the first part of *Rouze Up O Young Men of the New Age!* I wrote about a period when Hikari refused to do as he was told and used his superior size and strength to terrorize his brother and sister. Unfortunately, my account of it has been misconstrued, and I would like to clear this up. Even when Hikari hurt his sister, the person he loves most in all the world, his mind was reacting to painful, uncontrollable urges that welled up inside him rather than from any desire to hurt. Once the outburst had passed, moreover, he would spend the rest of the day with his head hanging down in shame, to the point where all of us, his sister included, felt a need to cheer him up. I stress this here because later a Catholic priest, known as a social activist, used this episode in the book—which he may simply have heard about, not read—as material in a lecture that was eventually published, mentioning all our names. "Hikari," he said, "beats his disabled friends with a stick," a fact from which he apparently derived some sort of moral lesson. But it was Hikari's own brother and sister he was beating, and it was done against his own wishes, under the influence of impulses he could neither understand nor resist. Quite possibly he may have thought at some point that what he was doing wasn't as serious as all that because it was just a family matter; but that didn't prevent him from feeling absolutely miserable after the event—perhaps because it *was* a family matter.

As for the rest of us, we parried the attacks as best we could, telling ourselves that it was one of our own who was delivering the blows. Sometimes we were angry, and sometimes forgiving, and sometimes ashamed of ourselves. It should be clear, however, that there is all the difference in the world between a family's internal behavior and the charge that Hikari had been assaulting people who weren't that close to him.

## 3

At last the day of our departure arrived, and we set out for Europe full of expectations and, to be honest, misgivings to match. I made my preparations much more cheerfully for this trip than for previous ones; Hikari seemed calmer than usual; and my wife was very much her normal self. By chance our departure fell on the drizzly morning of the ninth of June, the day on which the crown prince got married.

As we took our seats on the Swissair jumbo jet, my wife and I couldn't help feeling a certain nostalgia for the days when we'd made frequent trips around Japan with Hikari. He had been the rare sort of child who sat properly in his seat, whether on a plane or a train, and never squirmed or fidgeted until we arrived at our destination. In those days, going to the toilet was for him the most momentous of responsibilities, and when, in transit, he had taken it into his head to go, he set out on his mission with incredible intensity of purpose. Accordingly, whenever he first got on board, he carefully checked the whereabouts of the toilet, much as other people make a mental note of the emergency exits.

On this flight to Europe, we found, very little had changed. Though he was almost thirty years old, he still did his reconnoitering; then, after strapping himself in, he sat like a mannequin, hardly budging. However, once the plane had reached its cruising altitude and they began circulating trays of food, he ate his way slowly and methodically but almost endlessly—salmon, caviar-filled crepes, and so on—through everything on his tray. Eventually, when the lights in the cabin were turned down for a movie, Hikari lowered the back of his seat and appeared to fall asleep. At the beginning of the flight, he and I had been sitting side by side, but when he spilled some tea on his seat, I gave him mine and moved to an empty seat across the aisle.

I had been reading the whole time, but as the cabin settled down after the movie I realized that my wife, in the seat in front of us, had long since gone to sleep, no doubt exhausted from the effort to get us there. A bit later, however, it became apparent that Hikari, who hadn't so much as stirred in his seat, was in fact awake. As I watched him, though, I felt it was unlikely that he was brooding about this momentous journey he was on, and told myself that for him the anticipation was probably no more than what he would have felt on the big rented bus leaving for an overnight trip with his friends from the training center. With his eyes hidden behind a sleeping mask, he was listening through the headphones to the classical music channel of the plane's audio program, which he'd tuned in to almost as soon as he had reached his seat. Suddenly, he slid the mask down and his wise, dark eyes popped open, his face frozen in an image that I will never forget.

The greatest joy in Hikari's life is classical music, and no matter what it is, he never misses a chance to listen to it. You might almost say he *has* to listen. However, that day it seemed to go beyond the usual pattern, beyond anything that could be explained by mere curiosity. He had listened through the meal and through the film, and he went right on listening— to a tape-loop that by now he must have heard many times over. When we were planning the trip, Hikari had shown little interest in the maps of Europe or the pictures of hotels; instead he spent several days poring over schedules, working out a musical program for us in Salzburg, Vienna, and in Paris, where we would be stopping on our way home. All the while, however, he had been utterly calm and composed and had never betrayed the least excitement or agitation. Still, we were fairly certain that his parents' private misgivings about the journey had been passed on to him; and now, as he sat on this jumbo jet hurtling toward Europe, with his eyes wide open in the dim cabin light, he was facing—perhaps without quite realizing it still—an unprecedented adventure. It was no surprise, then, that he should cling for comfort to the one thing he had to depend on in life: music. From the time he was a small child, we have felt that when Hikari listens to music he passes over into a realm where neither my wife nor I can reach him and is absorbed into some sort of profound knowledge. It was with the wise eyes of such moments (wise despite the fact that his intelligence level wouldn't normally allow one to say this about him) that he now stared into the immediate future, steeling himself for what was to come. . . .

# Seiji Ozawa's Chair

BEFORE TAKING the morning train from Chur, which arrived in Salzburg in the early afternoon, the three of us went for a stroll in the courtyard of our hotel. Small, dark birds were singing shrilly in the neat copse of horse chestnuts, oaks, elms, and white birches that was tucked in next to the veranda, and in the tall trees of the forest that rose beyond. Hikari stared up into the branches trying to get a glimpse of them. This was the first sign of interest he had shown in birds since the day long ago when he'd abruptly lost the obsession of an autistic child with the sounds they made. It seems the excitement of the trip and this encounter with a new and unusual bird had revived the old fascination. As I went through the names of some of the birds I could remember from his old record, asking him if any resembled this one's high-pitched call, he silently shook his head after each name. Though there are times when Hikari will answer a question quite sharply and directly, there is generally a trick to holding a conversation with him that involves working in the same question a number of times while taking care not to irritate him. When I asked if it was like a robin, however, he spoke up with a smile: "... Except that the pitch is different!" This was his way of acknowledging the difference between European and Japanese birds.

Once on board the Eurocity International Express, he sat perfectly still, absorbed in the forests, buildings, and mountains that passed our window—above all, in the sudden appearance of the high Alpine peaks. I, for my part, remembered the travel diaries by Montaigne, Rabelais, and other Renaissance figures I had read when editing Professor Watanabe's works, which had given me an image of a dazzling, complex sequence of Protestant and Catholic cities on their itineraries, a procession that now came to life in the spires and mosque-like domes outside the window. To my wife, the two of us must have seemed mesmerized by the scenery.

Hikari can make himself at home almost anywhere, even on a long train ride; and so, taking our cue from him, we settled down to our own pastimes. I read, looking up from time to time for long enough to take in the range of indigenous trees we passed. My wife, on her side, waited for the train to reach a meadow before pressing her forehead to the window, straining to see the flowering plants and shrubs. Hikari, above and beyond our mundane curiosity, was "listening" to the scenery. All three of us were traveling in much the same way as we'd passed through the last thirty years. From the very beginning, whenever Hikari was confronted with some difficulty, we had all joined forces to help him overcome it; then, once the problem was dealt with, we would naturally go back to our own concerns and projects—never, however, allowing ourselves to drift too far apart, always remaining a family.

2

In Salzburg we were to stay at a hotel on the outskirts of town called the Kobenzl. Arriving at the nondescript station, we were taken straight up to the hotel, which from the outside looked like a rather modest mountain villa, perched at a height of about two thousand feet above sea level. Once we were settled in our rooms, however, we discovered the attraction of the place: the magnificent views of the city below our veranda. Directly in front of us we could see the old and new districts of the city lining the banks of the Salzach River. To the right were lush, dark green mountains, and to the left the snow-capped peaks of the Alps along what must have been the German border. As we stood there gazing at the Höhensalzburg range which filled the center of our view, the light faded and it began to rain. A pinkish lightning streaked the sky and thunder could be heard rumbling in the distance. Sleepless from jet-lag, I spent much of that night, until the first signs of dawn, staring out the window, watching as the clouds of a Renaissance engraving streamed in to cover the mountains.

I had been thinking about taking up the subject of meteorological oddities in the novel I was then writing, for which I was making notes and reading background material while we traveled. From my reading, I knew enough to be fairly certain that the weather conditions that spawn clouds are much the same in Europe and Japan. Nevertheless, when looking at classical paintings, I had often had the feeling that the clouds depicted in them are manifestly and peculiarly European in nature; and now here I was in Europe gazing at just such clouds. The skillful novelist, moreover—Balzac or Dickens, for example—can make me feel that some effect of the weather they're describing comes right out of my own experience, that the storm is one I have witnessed myself or the tranquil sky that follows it is one I have seen somewhere before.

As I said, it began to rain toward evening on our first day in Salzburg, and a breeze had come up as well. In general, the weather was chilly for the season and rain continued to fall on and off throughout our visit—not the normal state of affairs in that city, I'm sure. Still, slightly giddy from the excitement of the journey, we decided to ignore the weather and have our supper at a table set out under an awning on the wide veranda. Judging from the drawings my wife made of this scene in her oversized notebook, her attention was divided equally between the flowering plants in pots lining the veranda and the serious expression on Hikari's face as he sat, all dressed up, eating his meal.

The woman who ran the hotel gave the impression of being just the sort of person whose establishment would be known throughout Europe for its food, while remaining quite cozy and welcoming as well. Her husband, a large man with the air of a retired military officer, seemed somehow made of slightly coarser stuff; still, he was driving a rather smart car when he passed us with a wave one day as we were out on a long walk to pick some wild flowers. With their son and daughter-in-law, who were usually manning the front desk, we began to exchange greetings and hold short conversations, and they impressed us as serious, friendly people. Behind the desk was a photograph of Richard Nixon who, I remembered reading in a newspaper long ago, had been engulfed in a mob of demonstrators in Salzburg on a visit to ostensibly neutral Austria. When I asked the young man operating the switchboard about the photo, he said that he personally had been one of the demonstrators and that they had completely surrounded Salzburg airport. But he added that when Nixon had made his way through the crowd and arrived here at the hotel, he too had enthused about the food. . . .

We were also told that many of the musicians who came to Salzburg for the summer festival stayed here as well; and, indeed, when the dining room, which was jam-packed the weekend we arrived, finally quieted down a little, Hikari, who is quick to notice such things, spotted a chair with a nameplate on it marked "Seiji Ozawa." Ozawa, as it happened, was conducting Mahler's Third Symphony at a performance we caught at the end of our trip, a happy coincidence that came about as follows. My professor of French when I was a student had written critical biographies of a number of the members of the French royal family who were buried at the Cathedral of St. Denis on the outskirts of Paris, including Henri IV and Catherine de Médicis. Now it is said that during the French Revolution, after the tombs were dug up, parts of the royal remains—Henri's head, for instance, and Catherine's legs—were never returned but instead came into the possession of a private collector and were handed down from generation to generation. Professor Watanabe had written a grotesquely humorous essay investigating these claims, and it was no doubt under the influence of his peculiar tastes that I tacked on a visit to Paris at the end of our itinerary, for it coincided with the two-hundredth anniversary of the exhumation at St. Denis, and I wanted to see if there were any activities or publications commemorating the event. As it turned out, there was an arts festival being held at the cathedral, and I was able to get tickets for Ozawa's Mahler.

Years before, I had interviewed him when he first returned to Japan after his success in Europe, and I had always carried with me an impression of him as one of the best people of his age I'd ever met. More than thirty years later, seeing him on the stage they had set up in the cathedral, he seemed all the more impressive, perhaps because he was in his international element: conducting a French orchestra and chorus, an American soloist, and a local children's choir, all joining forces to bring a German composer's music to life.

During the long intermission after the first movement, Hikari proudly reminded us that he had eaten his dinner in the hotel in Salzburg in the chair marked "Seiji Ozawa."

3

Hikari's thirtieth birthday was celebrated at the Kobenzl in Salzburg, and for the occasion one of the people who had helped arrange our trip sent him a congratulatory fax. On it was a picture of a cake, which must have alerted the hotel owner to the fact that it was his birthday, since she, too, produced a present. My wife and I, in return, gave her a copy of Hikari's CD. All of this could be attributed to the normal sort of rapport that can develop between an innkeeper and guests who stay longer than a few days. The next morning, however, when we passed through the lobby, the young people behind the desk were even friendlier than usual, and the owner herself came to our table at lunch bubbling with excitement:

"We listened to your son's CD several times last night," she began, and then launched into a story. "You see, my father was the manager of a small hotel, and I was fortunate enough to marry a man who inherited this old place. We in our turn, I think, have made a success of the hotel, and our children seem willing to carry on the work with the same pride and affection—you've seen our son working with his wife at the front desk. Not only that, our grandchildren are growing up healthy and active, too. . . . And do you know what I attribute all this happiness to? To a lesson my father taught me: he said to always live life with a positive attitude . . . which is why I felt I just had to tell you that we think the way you and your wife treat your son is a wonderful example of that. We'd been talking about it as a family even before; but now that we've heard your son's music, we can see it even more clearly. His work is so pure and yet so personal," she said in closing. "What wonderful things can happen in music—and in life, too—can't they?!"

Very early on the morning of our departure, this woman and the young couple at the front desk were up (apparently at an even earlier hour than usual), and we all had our picture taken together, Hikari in a Tyrolean jacket. "You are a nice boy," she told him in her labored but warmhearted English.


4

During our week in Salzburg, followed by three days in Vienna, and then afterward in Paris, we were constantly surrounded by music. We heard concerts of all sorts: some played on ancient instruments, others performed in the costumes of Mozart's day. We visited musical museums for a puppet version of *The Magic Flute* or to see scores written in Mozart's or Beethoven's own hands. We even took a drive out of town to visit the little church where "Silent Night" is said to have been composed by the parishioners; and in every case Hikari seemed to be fascinated by what we were seeing and to enjoy himself most of all of us. Moreover, from early on in our stay in Salzburg, he began to spend time in front of the fireplace in the hotel, bent over his score paper hard at work on a new piece.

Some time ago I wrote something to the effect that there is a time in life when, after an extraordinary experience, one generally has the feeling that it will happen again, perhaps more than once. When this optimistic time has passed, however, we reach the point where even the most wonderful experiences bring with them the realization that they will never come again. In the autumn of one's life, such thoughts cast a shadow over even the happiest moments. On this journey as well, my wife and I couldn't help feeling something of this sort, though at the same time we were grateful for the experience. Wondering, now, what Hikari must have been feeling on his side, I get out the pictures from the trip: in most he appears almost indifferent, devoid of emotion, except for the ones where he is listening to music. . . .

As I mentioned before, even for short periods of time on board a plane or a train, Hikari tends to settle in and make himself at home; given a week or so at a hotel, he becomes totally acclimatized. The most certain sign that he has put down roots, however, is his habit of finding a little table, or just a bit of the floor to flop down on, where he can work on his composing. From this I would draw the following conclusion: that the thing that gives him the most complete sense of "home" is the time he spends composing music; or, to put it the other way around, his music is itself the expression of that feeling.

As for me, I wonder if I haven't been writing novels all these years as an expression of this same most basic feeling: that I, too, am at home in this world. Moreover, though I dream of finding a way in my writing to express something that transcends this world, it is in Hikari's music that I most often get a premonition of a world beyond our own.

# The Look of a Voice

WHEN THE TIME came to make a second CD of Hikari's more recent compositions, we decided to add a violin, and so we spent some time as a family comparing recordings of young violinists—and what an amazing crop of talent we discovered! It often seems to me that the future of my own country is growing murkier and more misguided by the day; but as I listened to these people play, I came to the conclusion that in terms of number and quality of musicians, at least, Japan is probably destined to be a leader.

Eventually, an outstanding young violinist named Tomoko

Kato was added to the previous duo. Hikari was, of course, the most avid listener to her recordings. When his mother and the producer of the CD had asked him his impression of them, he said that he felt her playing was very beautiful, before adding: "But I don't know what this person's voice looks like." At first everyone imagined he was referring to a particular quality of violin tone, but though Hikari's ordinary speech is generally fairly simple, when he is talking about music he tends to be quite technical and exact. So it turned out he was indeed referring to the fact that he hadn't heard her voice, and it seemed to be bothering him.

What does a voice look like? Not a bad question. In a sense, one could say that a person doesn't really have a voice per se, just the "appearance" of a voice. When we try to remember the sound of someone's voice, it isn't really the voice itself we try to retrieve from our memory but rather the way it "looked" on some particular occasion. But there was one other factor behind Hikari's comment: he has a visual impairment that makes it hard for him to distinguish certain objects even when he is wearing glasses, and as a result, for example, he often sits right next to the television screen in order to watch the Sumo wrestling and other favorite programs. However, since faces and expressions—what people "look" like—are so difficult for him to make out, he seems to have developed the habit of using his keen hearing to discern a person's character from the "look" of their voice.

That day, as we discussed Hikari's comment among ourselves, we all seemed to be suddenly paying closer attention to the sound of our own and others' voices, as if hearing them for the first time. And that reminded me of a story. Running straight north from our local station is a wide road lined with cherry trees which we go to look at every year when they are in full bloom, and if you follow that road to the end and wander a bit off to the right, you come to the house where the novelist Shohei Ooka once lived. It happened that Ooka used to phone our house from time to time, and when Hikari answered, Ooka, who was a wonderfully kind person, would engage him in conversation. Now Hikari is almost always eager to answer the telephone, except when he is recovering from a seizure, perhaps, and he is particularly fond of callers who have something nice to say to him before he passes the phone on, a category in which Ooka stood out as a model example. One day, however, after giving me the phone, Hikari went into the kitchen and announced to his mother: "Mr. Ooka is a note low today!"—an observation he repeated to me after I'd hung up. Having perfect pitch, Hikari had memorized the "look" of Ooka's voice in those terms, and on that particular day had noticed that it was slightly off-key. The strange, and sad, conclusion to this story is that Ooka had been calling to tell me that he was going into the hospital for some tests and wouldn't be able to read my new book which had just arrived. And that very afternoon, at the hospital, he had a heart attack and died. . . .

Hikari, who loves to hear stories in which he figures prominently, had listened intently when I reminded the family of this episode. I then turned to ask him a question:

"Hikari, do you still remember Mr. Ooka's voice? Not the low one you heard that day but his normal voice?"

"I still remember it, because I heard it again recently," he answered.

At this, my wife and daughter started to laugh, supposing that by "recently" Hikari meant five or six years ago, but I preferred to take it to mean that he had heard him as one sometimes hears people in a dream; and what a good thing it would be if this odd comment of his meant that he had, in fact, heard Ooka's gentle, encouraging voice again. And what a good and profoundly heartening thing it would be in all our lives if, from time to time, we too could hear the voices of those who have left us.

2

In conjunction with the release of Hikari's new CD, which was to be called *The Music of Hikari Oe: 2* (CO 78953), friends and acquaintances proposed a number of projects. Among them was a plan to make a television film documenting the relationship between Hikari's life and music and my own literary activities, a proposal we decided to accept since it seemed that the film might serve a wider purpose in describing the path taken by a disabled person toward self-expression and the ways in which a family can affect that process.

So it was, then, that as the filming drew closer, Hikari and I decided to do what we could to prepare ourselves, each in his own way. Part of the plan was to have him talk about various aspects of his life on camera, and for this we wanted him to practice speaking carefully into a tape recorder at home, trying to remember as much as he could, especially from his childhood. Facing the microphone, he was tense, anxious to get the answers right, adopting an unusually formal, almost ceremonious tone of voice. As I listened, I was made aware of the extent to which even in everyday conversation he was careful to give a certain rhythm and overall shape to his speech. For Hikari, with his particular disability, this form and texture seem to be the fundamental principles of speech. Indeed, even when the sense of what he is saying is unclear and his syntax falls to pieces, he tends to preserve the same pattern of intonation from the beginning of his sentence to the end; in other words, for him the important thing is not so much the sense but the musicality of human speech, or, as he would put it, "the look of a voice."

All of which gives rise to another thought. It is often said that the novels and essays produced by Hikari's father are difficult to read; blunter critics have claimed they are poorly written. This, over time, has become something of an accepted fact—one, moreover, that I feel is largely true. But it is only recently that I've begun to realize that the source of the problem can perhaps be traced to my losing a sense of the music in the human voice. At the time I first began writing fiction, only five or six years had elapsed since I'd left my home in Shikoku—about the same amount of time at present since Ooka's death, a period in which Hikari has continued to remember our friend's voice, right down to its particular pitch. By the same token, I think, during those first few years away from home, the local speech patterns back there continued to be the most basic and natural ones to me, while the cadences of Tokyo speech had much the same feeling as a foreign language. Thus I developed the (rather self-conscious) tendency to focus on the written word to the exclusion of the way it sounds, with the result that my writing style, particularly in my early and middle works at least, has a peculiarly "constructed" quality to it.

But, taking this a stage further, I feel that by listening to the patterns and tones of Hikari's speech over the years, I have somehow come to understand the importance of the human voice, have somehow been cured of my problem—a theory that I would someday like to put to the test in a novel. . . .

### 3

A week of these practice interviews had a noticeable effect on Hikari's way of speaking. By the end of it he was even using polite forms of speech when he answered a phone call from Dr. K of the neuropsychology department of his hospital, who rang to ask if I would be interested in adding a novelist's point of view to a conference that was being organized to consider a pressing problem facing doctors in his field: namely, that of providing counseling and therapy for the growing number of foreign workers in Japan who experience psychological difficulties triggered by cultural differences. Rather than going into further detail after I'd agreed, however, the doctor seemed intent on telling me, with obvious pleasure, how surprised he had been when Hikari had answered the phone but even more surprised at how well he spoke. Moreover, the next time Hikari went to the hospital for his regular checkup and medication, he was again praised for the progress he was making. Right at the end of his appointment, though, he had apparently answered the doctor's questions with one of his own: "Next month, which is April, will be so kind to continue?"

Now, this is typical of him—to leave out the most important element in his question: *what* it is that's to continue. No doubt *he* knows what he has already formulated in his mind—in this case, a point connected with the fact that several of his teachers at the training center were leaving shortly, at the end of March—so he seems to feel there is no need to spell it all out again. This can work perfectly well when he is speaking to someone—my wife, for instance—who already knows his mind; in fact, in cases where a background of mutual understanding exists between people, this sort of abbreviated conversation can save a great deal of time and effort. It even has a name: "strategically stylized" speech, as the theorist Kenneth Burke has dubbed it. The difference—and the problem—in Hikari's case, however, is that he uses these shortcuts in conversations where no such understanding applies. At such times, whoever is with him has to supply the missing links; and when this happens it is Hikari, as much as his interlocutor, who listens intently, nodding in satisfaction. The trouble is that our help in speeding up things like a doctor's interview may actually be slowing down his development, by depriving him of the need to make a linguistic effort.

All this goes to show, no doubt, that our sense of parental honor is still alive and well, despite the fact that we thought we'd long since lost any pretensions of that kind. But as I sat with Hikari, the microphone between us, trying to get him to speak as correctly as possible, waiting patiently for him to supply those often-deleted *whats* of his own accord, I had the feeling that I was watching dormant skills slowly coming to life.

# "It's Was All Awful"

SEEING OURSELVES on the TV screen when the documentary was broadcast was an opportunity to look at familiar relationships from unfamiliar angles. One episode showed Hikari and me on a visit to the Atomic Bomb Museum in Hiroshima. As we were about to enter a room featuring a model of the city immediately after the blast, Hikari seemed terrified, more so than I had ever seen him before. In the end I almost had to push him inside. After the tour, we sat down by a window in the hallway, both feeling drained, but after a while I pressed him for his impressions of what he'd just seen. "It's was all awful," he said quite force-fully without looking up, the answer half a groan and half an indictment.

I have watched this scene several times now on the video, and it seems strange to me that Hikari, whose vocabulary and syntax are sometimes a bit haywire but whose diction is always careful—he never lets himself speak sloppily—should have produced this garbled-sounding sentence. I think he meant it basically in the present tense, however: everything, from the emotions aroused by the photos and paintings of that summer of devastation, to even the sunset outside with the Peace Tower lit from behind—all of it "is awful." This may also have included the man sitting next to him, trying to keep up a cheerful front despite feeling exhausted and depressed himself. Or, possibly, the momentary hesitation between tenses may have suggested that "it was awful" of me to have forced him to go through all this, but that he now no longer felt that way.

After the program appeared, one of the weekly maga-zines, in its TV column, expressed opposition to the idea of making a film of disabled children for television; more spe-cifically, the writer—a woman—said that if she were the mother of a child like that she would never have allowed them to show him having an epileptic fit. Quite apart from various inaccuracies it contained about epilepsy, however, I felt the piece revealed not only the prejudice concealed in her apparent concern but the distance between her and an actual epileptic's mother, in whom years of living with this hardship would have bred a more tolerant attitude.

## 2

To coincide with the release of Hikari's second CD, a concert was organized. One morning just before it, we discovered a couple of postcards lying in the mud next to our mailbox after a night of rain. They were the cards that had been distributed at press conferences connected with the CD, showing a drawing of a water rail and part of a score in Hikari's hand. On one of them was an anonymous message written on a word processor; the other had apparently been tossed in with it as so much litter. They hadn't arrived with the regular mail, and it seemed unlikely that anyone would have come from any distance on a rainy night to deliver them, so we were left with the feeling that they were the work of someone in the neighborhood. The message read as follows:

> If Hikari Oe weren't the son of Kenzaburo Oe, would his works be performed at a major concert hall? Would they have been released on a CD at all? And would you have had the cooperation of some of the best-known performers in Japan (who, nevertheless, don't measure up to international standards)? It's like "The Emperor's New Clothes": a bit of transparent music, held up by a sense of civic duty. Which is all very nice for you. But I'd like you to know that there are countless discontented composers out there who can't get their music

noticed despite real talent. And I'd like you to know what most experts really think of your son's music!

My response to this card came in the form of a short talk I gave before the concert started:

> The person whose works you will be hearing today is someone who has never cried; someone also who may never have had a dream. I suppose for parents who have normal, healthy children, not dreaming wouldn't appear to be a matter of any great concern, but for us it seemed painfully clear that something important was missing in our son's life. Which is perhaps why we spent so much time and effort trying to teach him what it meant to dream. . . . "After you've had your evening medicine and you get into bed," we'd say, "you go to sleep, right? Well, suppose a kangaroo were suddenly kneeling by your bed, and it took your hand in its paw and started sniffing you. . . . That would be a dream!" But Hikari would look away, obviously put out, and say: "I don't think there are any kangaroos around here."
>
> Hikari and dreams, we decided sadly, were incompatible. You will find, however, that among the works included on his second CD is one called "Dream," a title he gave it himself. Has Hikari begun to dream, then? Or is this music something that welled up inside him in his attempt to imagine the thing his parents were always talking about? When we tried to get him to answer this question himself, he was, in his usual way, enigmatic.
>
> The voice you hear in this work for violin and piano

is one we hadn't heard before: a voice I would describe as that of "a wailing soul." But is it one that comes from the sort of dreams he has, or from what he only thinks of as a dream? Where *does* this unhappy voice come from? From deep inside him—that much one knows for sure—and it can in fact be heard throughout his new collection. And far from being in opposition to the pure, radiant sound of his earlier CD, it is inextricably linked with it. It represents a development, a deepening of his art.

Whether in the field of music or literature, creating a work of art is the act of bringing order to something that hitherto was chaotic, giving form to something that was vague and undefined. The freshness that attracts us to the work of a young artist comes from the encounter with a first, emergent form. We feel that we have met a whole new human being. This was the feeling that Hikari's first CD gave, I think. But one of the things that distinguish human beings from animals is their need, having once created a certain form, to build on it, to go one step further and elaborate on it or transform it altogether. And that is exactly what you see at work in my son's second collection. In practice, he listened to his first CD over and over again, learning from it and reshaping it, with the result that the techniques he uses have become much more diverse, the expression richer and more resonant.

Hikari has no verbal means of describing this experience, but it is safe to say that his exploration brought him into contact with a solid core of sorrow that had collected in his heart, and by cutting through it he released this other sound, the voice of "a wailing soul."

This pattern of development, however, has wider implications in the realm of art in general, and my own work is perhaps a good example of it. I began writing fiction as a student in Tokyo. If I hadn't been exposed to the writing of a particular scholar of French literature when I was still in high school and felt drawn to study under him, I would probably have ended my days in my home village in the south, working for the forestry collective, just as my parents and their parents before them had. As it happened, though, I published a short story in the University of Tokyo newspaper. It is now thirty-seven years since that first piece of writing appeared, but I realize that I have spent them building on that initial form, remodeling, amplifying it. In the process, I discovered in myself layers of sorrow and pain that are darker and more complex than Hikari's; in fact, looking back on all my other books, I am shocked by the extent to which I have spent my life drawing out that darkness. . . .

But Hikari's recent music, particularly his "Dream" and "Nocturnal Capriccio," reveals another truth as well: that in the very act of expressing himself there is a healing power, a power to mend the heart. This power, moreover, isn't limited to him alone but extends to those receptive to what he has to express. And this is the miracle of art. For in the music or literature we create, though we come to know despair—that dark night of the soul through which we have to pass—we find that by actually giving it expression we can be healed and know the joy of recovering; and as these linked experiences of pain and recovery are added to one another, layer upon layer, not only is the artist's work enriched but its benefits are shared with others. . . .

Hikari may not be much good with words, but where music is concerned he has a carefully cultivated ability to concentrate, one that his mother and his teachers have helped him develop but which he himself has also honed by listening to recordings and the radio during almost every waking hour for more than twenty years. The French philosopher Simone Weil has written about this sort of concentration, asking what it is that could link such apparently disparate experiences as "study" and "the love of god," and concluding that "the key is in the fact that prayer is a matter of concentration. Prayer is the directing of all the attention of which the soul is capable toward god." And when I see my son giving all his powers of attention to his music, I am convinced that Weil was right. . . .

In the same passage, she writes of one of the legends concerning the Holy Grail: it seems that a certain knight, coming upon the gravely wounded king who was the guardian of the Grail, greeted him with the question "In what way are you suffering?" and in that very choice of words revealed himself as worthy of being the next bearer of the sacred vessel. In the same way, I feel the people who have most helped Hikari have approached him with the same inquiry. Among them, for example, are the performers in the concert you're about to hear— each of whom, moreover, has that same ability to concentrate on his or her own discipline. And I feel that you in the audience, too, who have gone to the trouble of coming here, are asking him as well, "In what way are you suffering?" And for each of you, my hope is that his music will serve as an answer.

3

As soon as I'd finished speaking the performance began, and when it finally came to a close the musicians beckoned for the composer to join them on the stage. On previous occasions, it had always been my job to escort him there, but I had asked my wife to do it at this and subsequent events. As the two of them made their way slowly down the aisle, he much taller and sturdier than she, his manner seemed to suggest that it was he who was escorting her rather than the other way around. They moved together toward the lighted stage, not stumbling at all as they went, and I watched them from my seat in the dark with a peaceful sense of accomplishment, as though I were seeing a scene in their life at some point in the future when it will be just the two of them.

# Afterword

by Yukari Oe

IN THE HIGHLANDS of North Karuizawa where we have spent our summers every year, there is a broad slope where wild flowers of all sorts bloom in great profusion: scabious, vetch, day lilies, and so on; and, being fond of flowers, I began making sketches of them with colored pencils when I was still quite young. Having watched me at this for many years, my husband suggested I do some drawings to illustrate the text of what eventually became *A Healing Family*.

These essays about our family life—for him, a rather rare

way of treating the subject—were first serialized in a quarterly magazine called *Sawarabi*, which has a medical focus. But though my husband welcomed the project as a chance to write about something connected with and of interest to the medical profession from the standpoint of the patient's family, I was initially reluctant. I thought it would be more than I could manage. When I was told that all they needed were some sketches of flowers and "snapshots" of the family, however, I set to work. That was over five years ago.

Recently, the Oes have had more than their share of big events: my mother's second hospitalization, the release of Hikari's second CD, concerts in that connection, our first trip abroad with Hikari in the wake of a rather severe seizure, the filming of an NHK documentary about us, and, of course, my husband's prize. The upshot of all this excitement, for me, was that I had almost no time to paint. Needless to say, I am a complete amateur, but it bothered me that I couldn't do more than a handful of second-rate sketches. Still, the people from the magazine were encouraging.

These sketches bring back some vivid memories: of drawing bean bags and paper balloons by my mother's hospital bed, for example, or of being shut in by the rain at our hotel in Salzburg, spending the whole day doing drawings of wild flowers in a cup while Hikari, who hadn't had a chance to write any music for a while, sat nearby, bent over his score. At one time, during our summers in the country, he had merely played at being a composer, just as I played at being an illustrator. Now, however, he had become the real thing, whereas I still seemed to be . . . well, playing at it. Never mind—I am glad at least I can make some contribution to this picture of our family life.